PIANO / VOCAL / GUITAR

rest in peace

40 Memorial Songs

ISBN 978-1-4234-7766-2

HAL•LEONARD®
CORPORATION

7777 W. BLUEMOUND RD. P.O. BOX 13819 MILWAUKEE, WI 53213

Visit Hal Leonard Online at
www.halleonard.com

contents

ANGEL

Words and Music by
SARAH McLACHLAN

Gently

Spend all your ___ time wait - ing
straight line,

for that sec - ond chance, ___ for a break that would make ___
and ev - 'ry - where you turn there's vul - tures and thieves ___

___ it o - kay. ___
___ at your ___ back. ___

There's al - ways some ___ rea - son
Storm keeps on ___ twist - ing.

Recorded a half step higher.

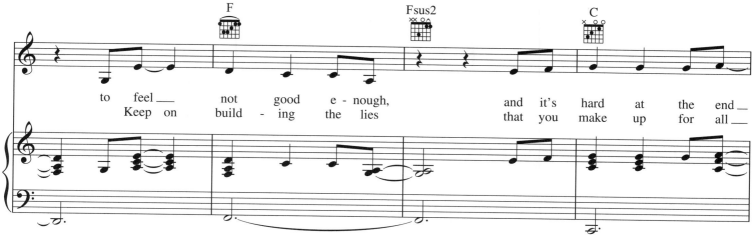

to feel ___ not good e - nough,
Keep on build - ing the lies

and it's hard at the end ___
that you make up for all ___

___ of the day. ___
___ that you lack. ___

I need some dis - trac - tion,
It don't make no dif - f'rence

oh, ___ beau - ti - ful re - lease. ___
es - cap - ing one last time. ___

Mem - o - ry
It's eas - i - er

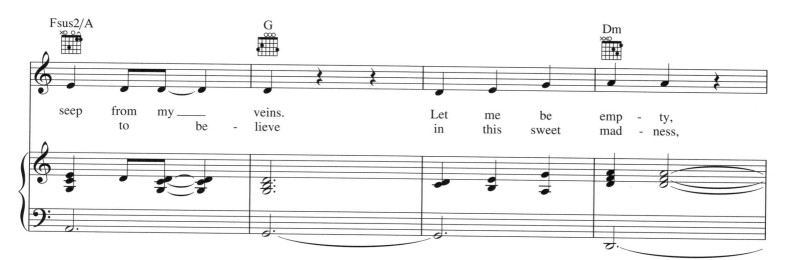

seep from my ___ veins.
to my be - lieve

Let me be emp - ty,
in this sweet mad - ness,

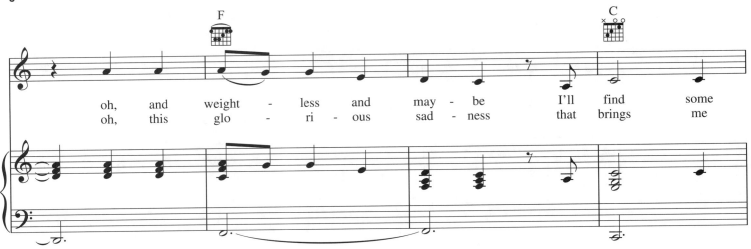

oh, and weight - less and may - be I'll find some
oh, this glo - ri - ous sad - ness that brings me

peace to - night _____ } in the arms of the an -
to my knees _____ }

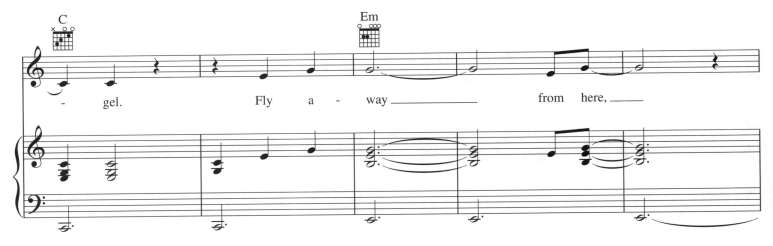

- gel. Fly a - way _____ from here, _____

from this dark, cold _____ ho - tel room

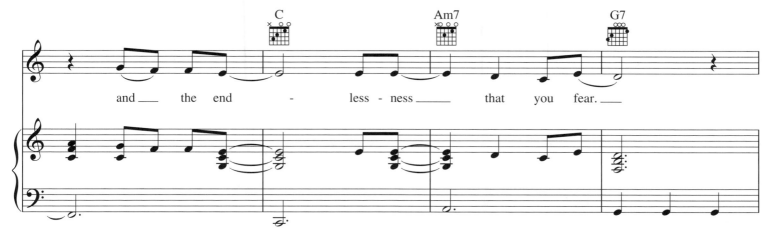

and ___ the end - less - ness ___ that you fear. ___

You are ___ pulled from ___ the wreck - age

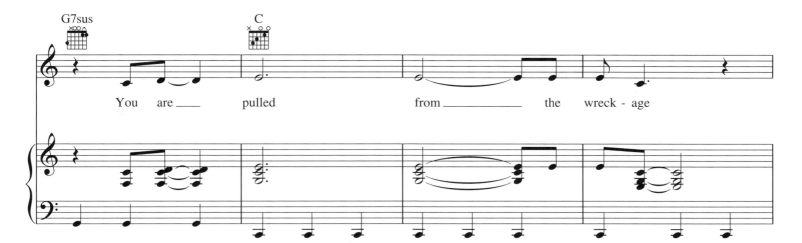

of your si - lent ___ rev - er - ie. ___

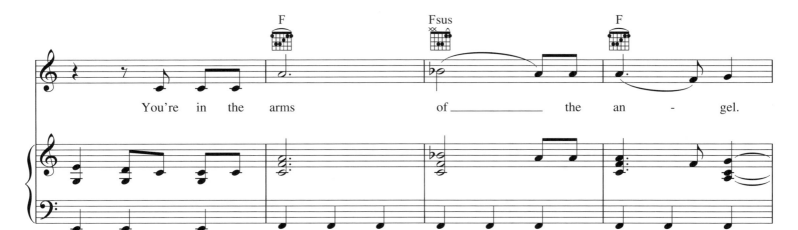

You're in the arms of ___ the an - gel.

To Coda ⊕

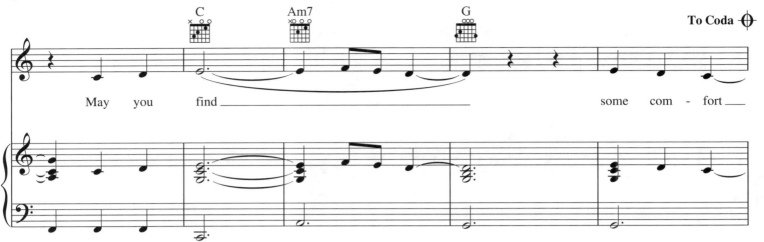

May you find _____ some com - fort _____

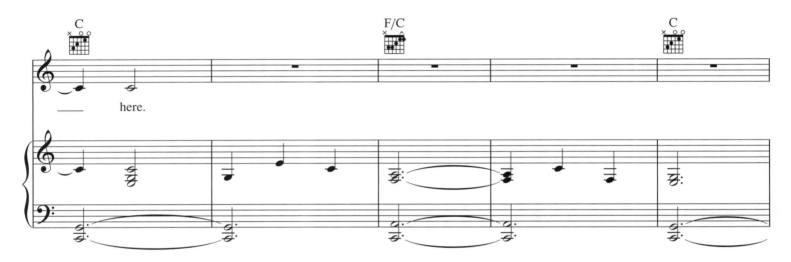

_____ here.

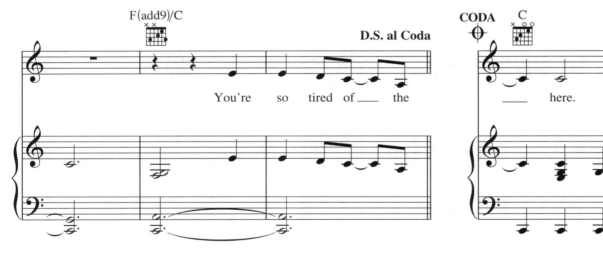

D.S. al Coda

You're so tired of ____ the

CODA ⊕

_____ here.

You're in the arms of _____ the

an - gel. May you find _____

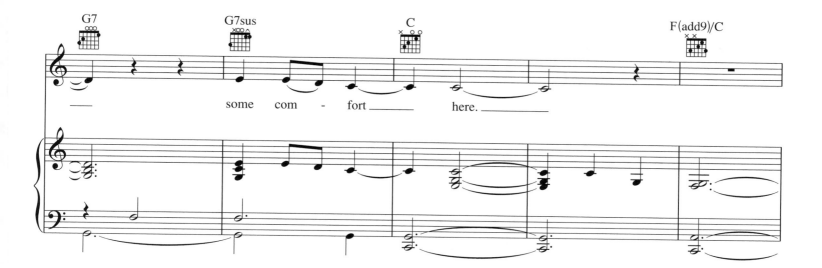

some com - fort _____ here. _____

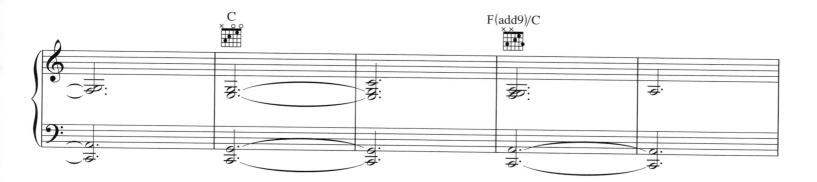

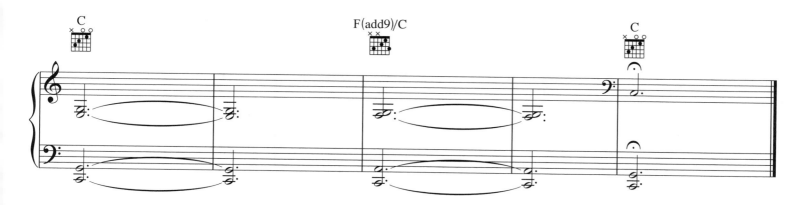

BURY ME

Words and Music by
DWIGHT YOAKAM

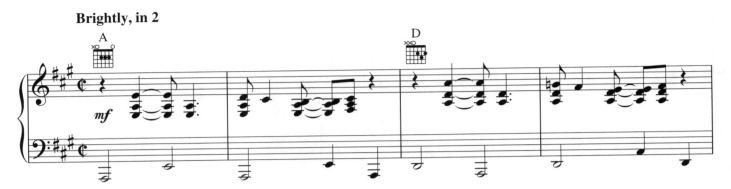

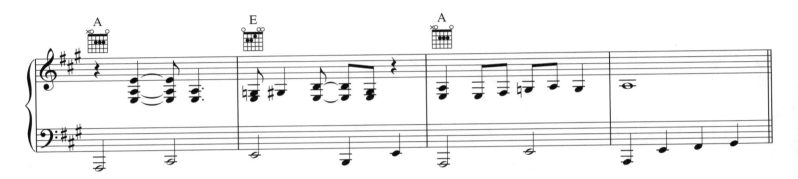

moun - tains. Rest ___ my ___

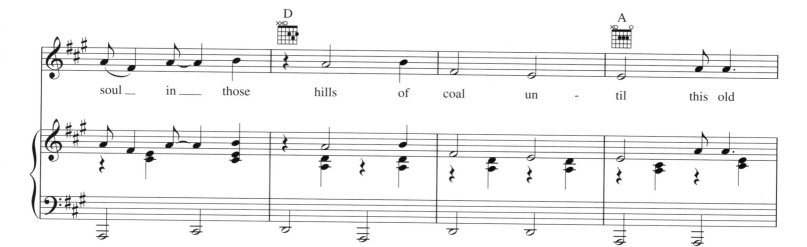

soul ___ in ___ those hills of coal un - til this old

earth does a - trem - ble. Now, don't ___ you

mourn ___ for me when my soul ___ is free. No,

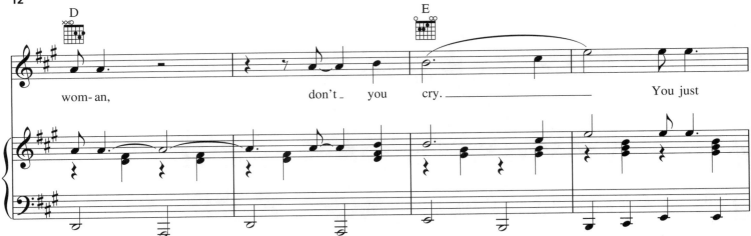

wom-an,   don't _ you   cry. _____   You just

bur - y   me _____   a - long   the   big

sand - y,   un - der a blue ___ Ken - tuck - y sky. ___

This old   town _____ of sin,   it's a - bout ___
came to _____ this land,   I was strong _

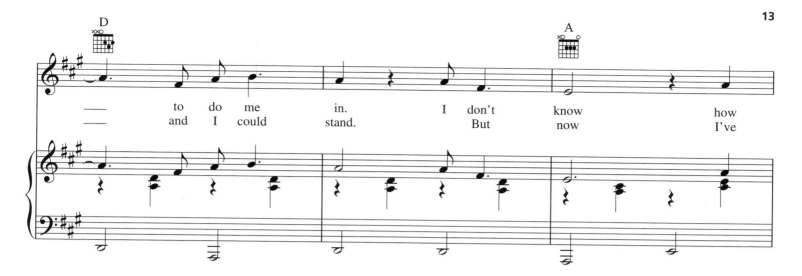

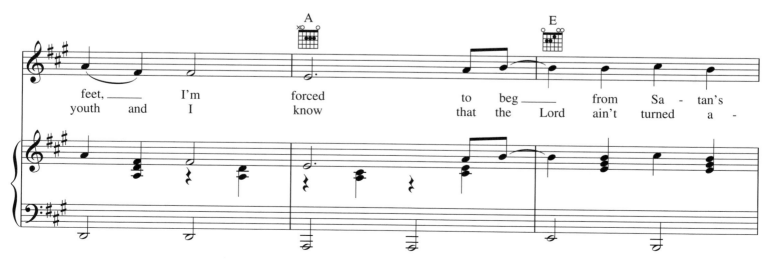

So bur - y me _____ a -

long the ___ big sand - y, down in those

blue ___ gray _____ moun - tains.

Rest _____ my ___ soul ___ in ___ those hills of

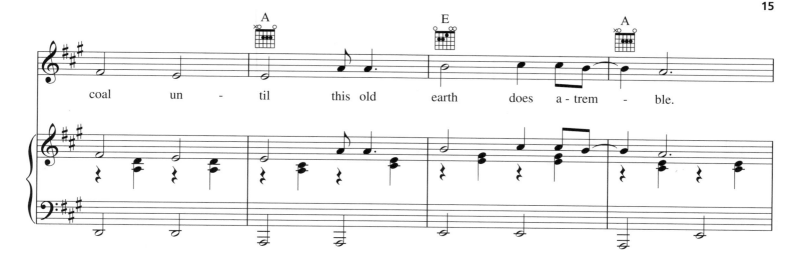

coal un - til this old earth does a - trem - ble.

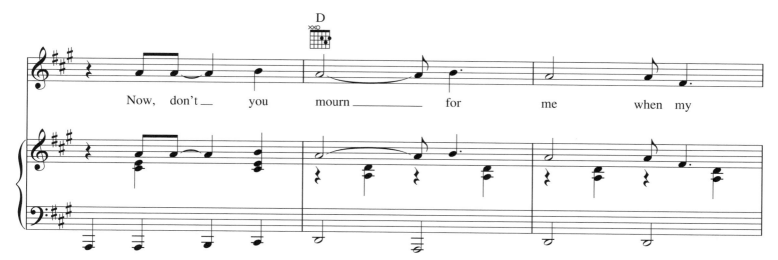

Now, don't __ you mourn _____ for me when my

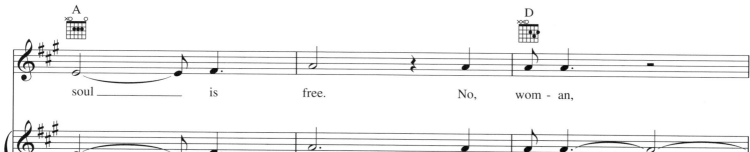

soul _____ is free. No, wom - an,

don't __ you cry. _____ You just

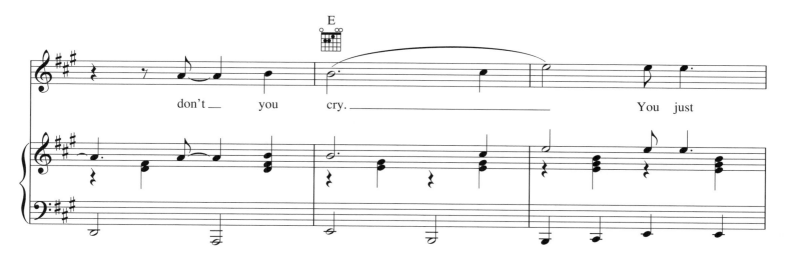

bur - y me _____ a - long the big

sand - y, un - der a blue ___ Ken - tuck - y sky. _

To Coda

When I

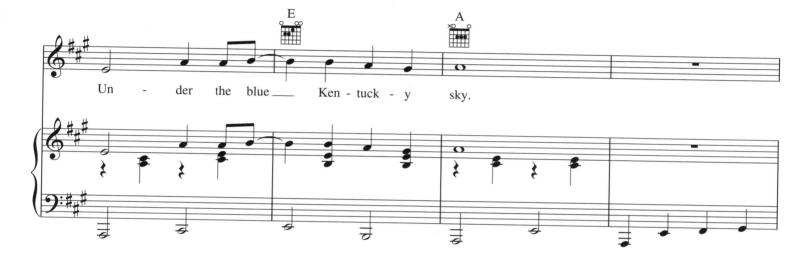

Un - der the blue ___ Ken - tuck - y sky.

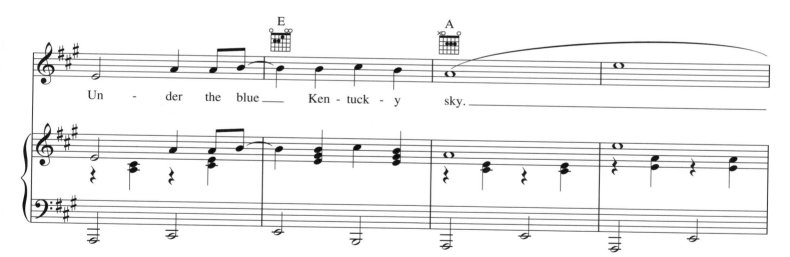

Un - der the blue ___ Ken - tuck - y sky. ___

BYE BYE

Words and Music by MARIAH CAREY,
MIKKEL S. ERIKSEN, TOR ERIK HERMANSEN
and JOHNTA AUSTIN

Ballad

This is for my peo-ple who just lost some-bod-y, your best friend, your ba - by, your

man — or your la - dy. Put your hand way up high, — we will nev - er

say bye. No, no, no. — Ma-mas, dad-dies, sis-ters, broth-ers, friends and cous-ins,

this is for my peo-ple who lost _____ their grand-moth-ers. Lift your head to the sky _____

_____ 'cause we will nev-er say bye. _____ As a child _____

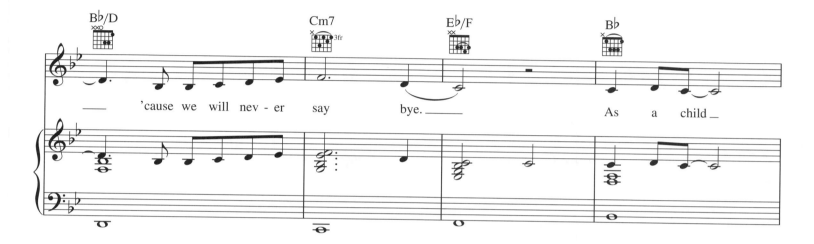

there were them times _____ I did-n't get _____ it but you kept me in line. _____ I did-n't

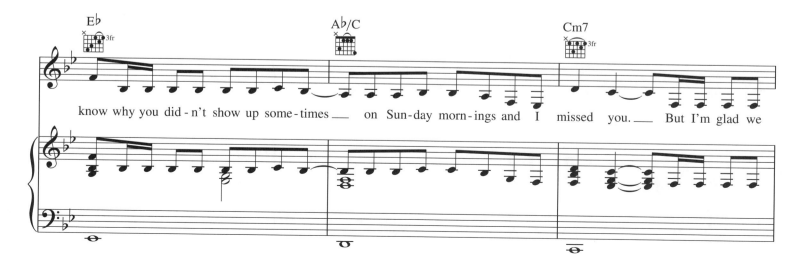

know why you did-n't show up some-times _____ on Sun-day morn-ings and I missed you. _____ But I'm glad we

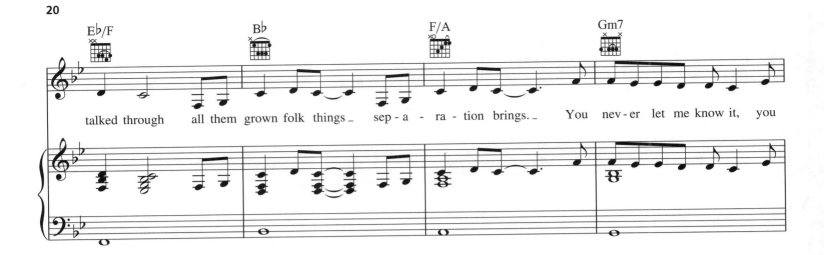

Miss you but I try not to cry as ___ time ___ goes ___ by. ___

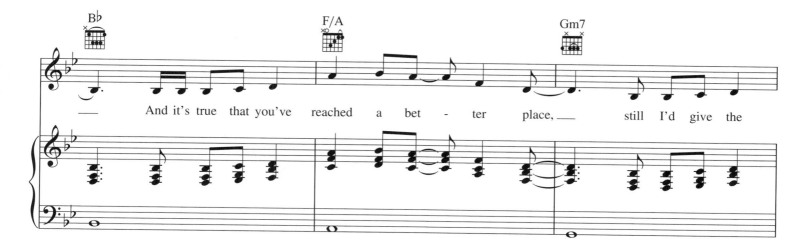

___ And it's true that you've reached a bet - ter place, ___ still I'd give the

world to see ___ your face. ___ And be right here next to you, but it's like you're gone too soon.

Now the hard - est thing to do is say ___ bye ___ bye. ___ Bye

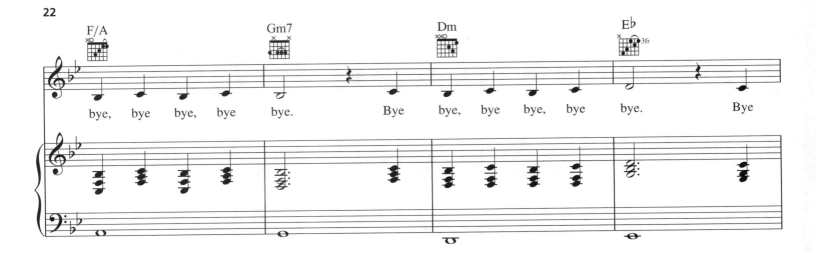

bye, bye bye, bye bye. Bye bye, bye bye, bye bye. Bye

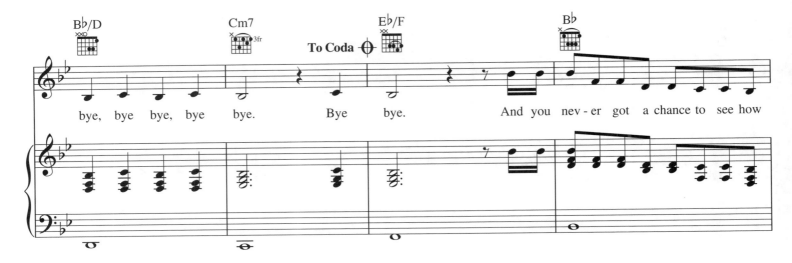

bye, bye bye, bye bye. Bye bye. And you nev - er got a chance to see how

good I've done, and you nev - er got to see me back at num - ber one. I

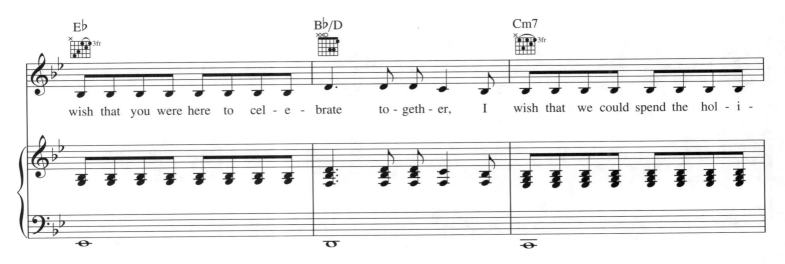

wish that you were here to cel - e - brate to - geth - er, I wish that we could spend the hol - i -

days to-geth-er. I re-mem-ber when you used to tuck me in at night with the

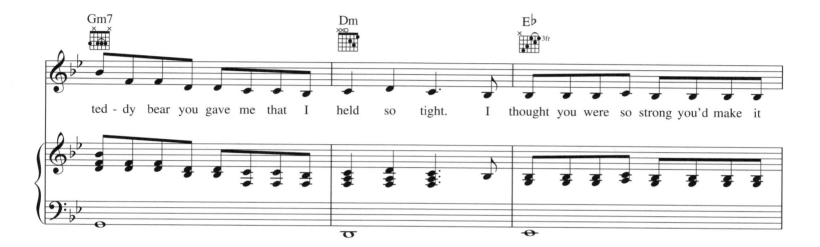

ted-dy bear you gave me that I held so tight. I thought you were so strong you'd make it

D.S. al Coda

through what-ev-er, it's so hard to ac-cept the fact you're gone for-ev-er. _____

CODA

bye. This is for my peo-ples who just lost some-bod-y, your

best friend, your ba - by, your man, __ or your la - dy. Put your hand way up high, __

__ we will nev - er say bye. No, no no. __ Ma - mas, dad - dies, sis - ters, broth - ers,

F/A   Gm7   Dm

friends and cous - ins, this is for my peo - ples who lost _____ their grand - moth - ers.

Eb   Bb/D   Cm7   Eb/F

Lift your head to the sky ___ 'cause we will nev - er say bye, _____ bye. __

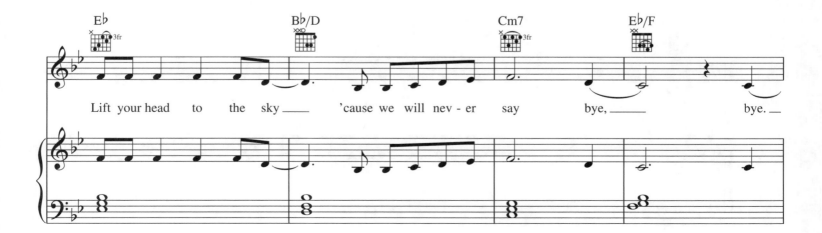

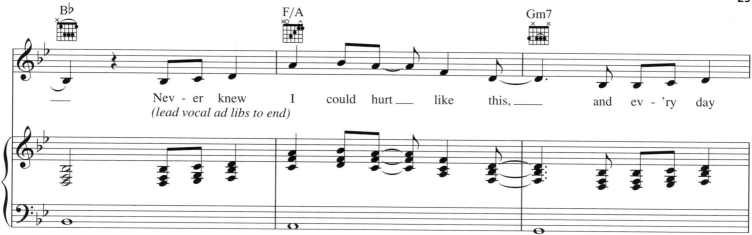

Nev - er knew I could hurt __ like this, __ and ev - 'ry day
(lead vocal ad libs to end)

life rolls on __ I wish __ I could talk to you for a while. Miss you but I try not to cry

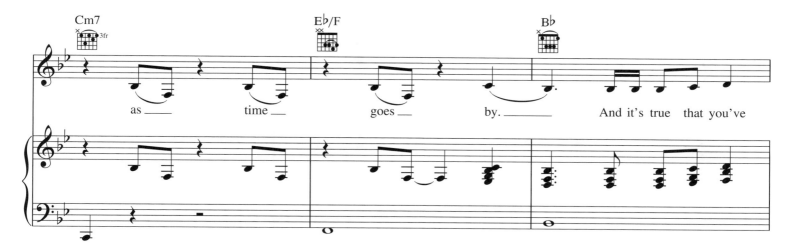

as __ time __ goes __ by. __ And it's true that you've

reached a bet - ter place, __ still I'd give the world to see __ your face. _

And be right here next to you, but it's like you're gone too soon.

Now the hard-est thing to do is say ___ bye ___ bye. ___ Bye

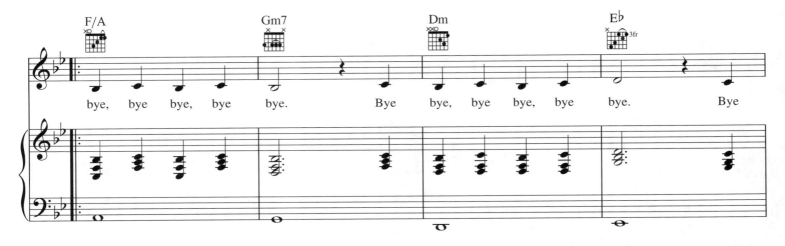

bye, bye bye, bye bye. Bye bye, bye bye, bye bye. Bye

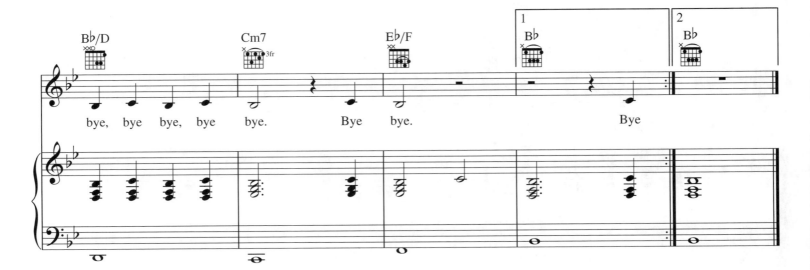

bye, bye bye, bye bye. Bye bye. Bye

DANCE WITH MY FATHER

Words by LUTHER VANDROSS
and RICHARD MARX
Music by LUTHER VANDROSS

Moderately slow

Back when I was a child, be - fore life re - moved all the in - no - cence,

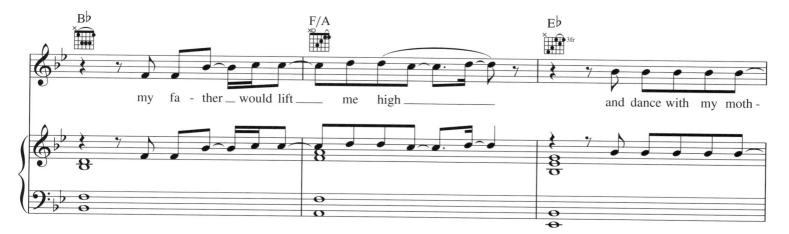

my fa - ther would lift me high and dance with my moth -

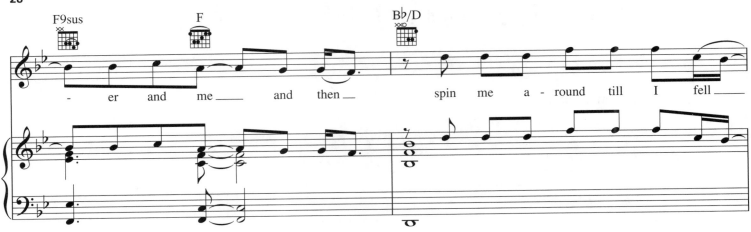

-er and me ___ and then ___ spin me a - round till I fell ___

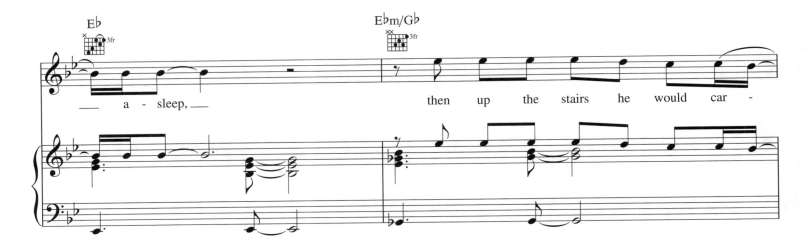

___ a - sleep, ___ then up the stairs he would car -

-ry me. ___ And I knew ___ for sure ___ I was loved. _

___ If I could get ___ an - oth - er chance, _ an -
I could steal ___ one fi - nal glance, _ one _

Gm　　　　　　Eb　　　　　　Cm

oth - er　walk, _　an - oth - er　dance _ with him, }
fi - nal　step, _　one　fi - nal　dance _ with him, }　　I'd play　a song that would nev -

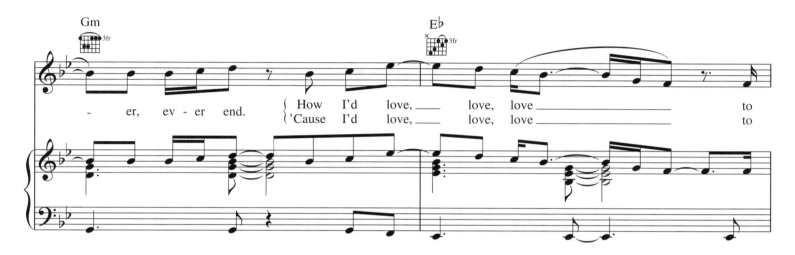

Gm　　　　　　　　　　　Eb

- er,　ev - er end.　{ How　I'd　love, ____　love, love _____　to
　　　　　　　　　　'Cause　I'd　love, ____　love, love _____　to

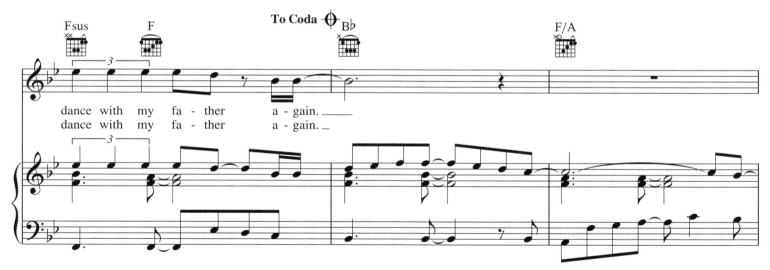

Fsus　　F　　　　**To Coda** ⊕ Bb　　　　　　F/A

dance with　my　fa - ther　a - gain. _____
dance with　my　fa - ther　a - gain. __

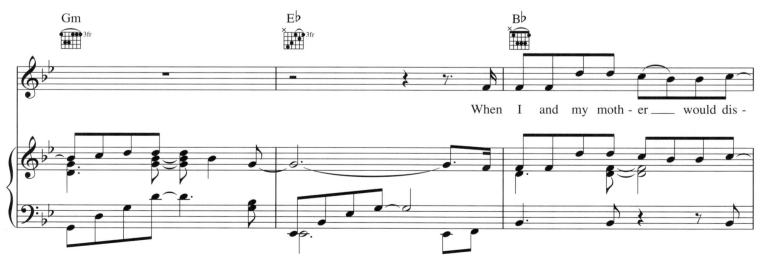

Gm　　　　　　Eb　　　　　　Bb

When　I　and　my　moth - er ____　would dis -

- a-gree, to get my way I would run___ from her___ to him.___

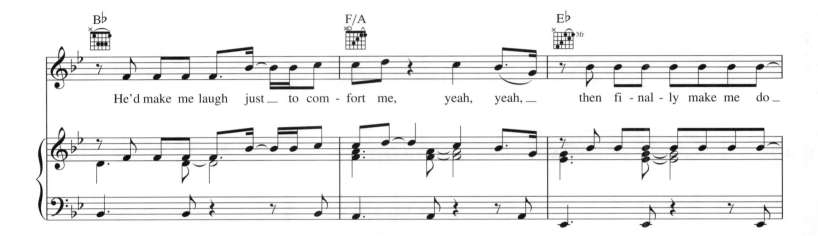

He'd make me laugh just___ to com-fort me, yeah, yeah,___ then fi-nal-ly make me do___

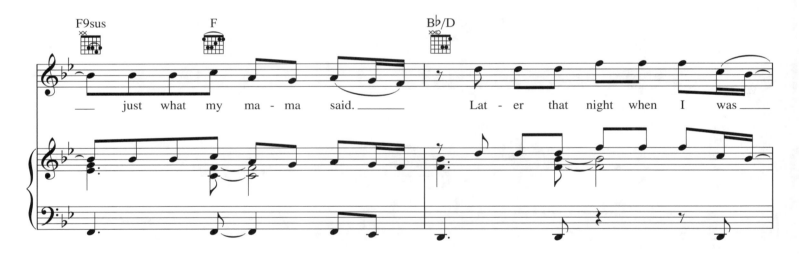

___ just what my ma-ma said._____ Lat-er that night when I was___

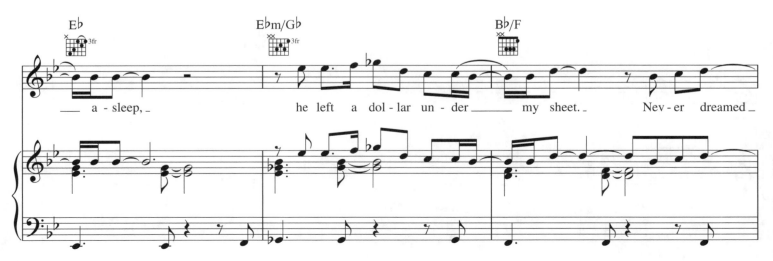

___ a-sleep,___ he left a dol-lar un-der_____ my sheet.___ Nev-er dreamed___

D.S. al Coda

that he _____ would be gone _____ from me. _____ If

CODA

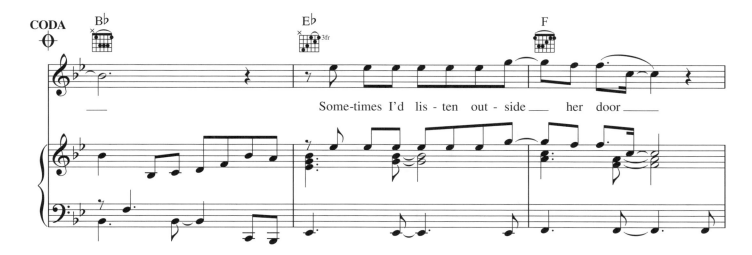

Some-times I'd lis-ten out-side ____ her door _____

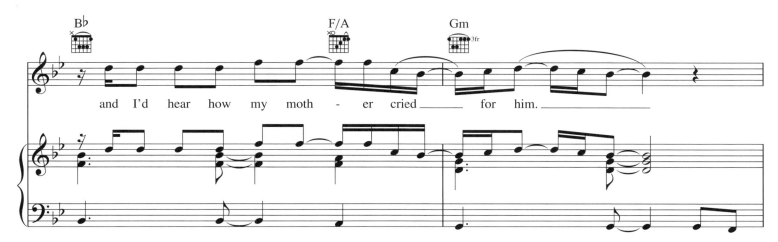

and I'd hear how my moth - er cried _____ for him. _____

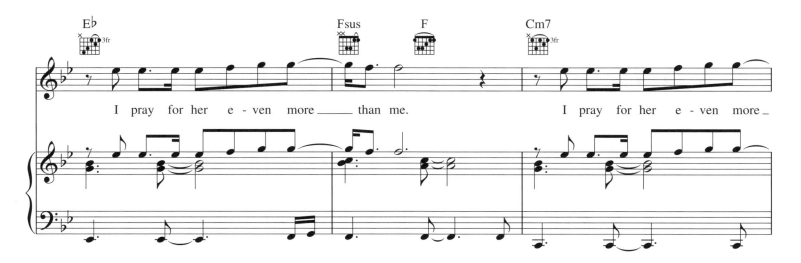

I pray for her e - ven more _____ than me.   I pray for her e - ven more__

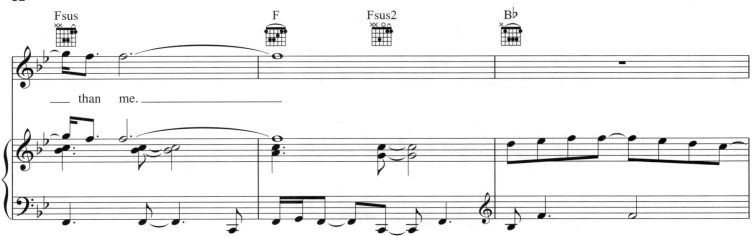

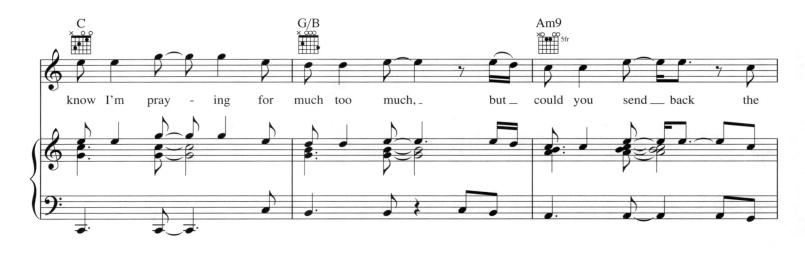

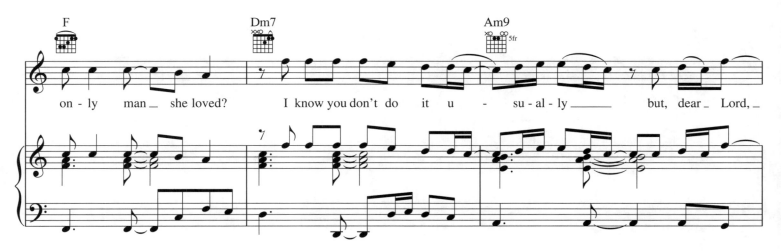

she's dy - ing _____ to dance with my fa - ther _____

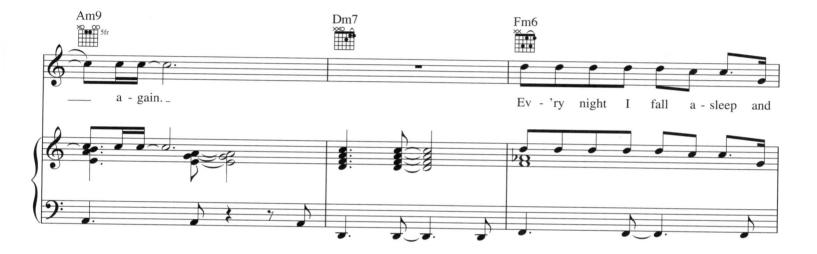

_____ a - gain. ___ Ev - 'ry night I fall a - sleep and

this is all I ev - er dream. ___

EVEN NOW

from LIES OF THE HEART

Words by JACK MURPHY
Music by FRANK WILDHORN

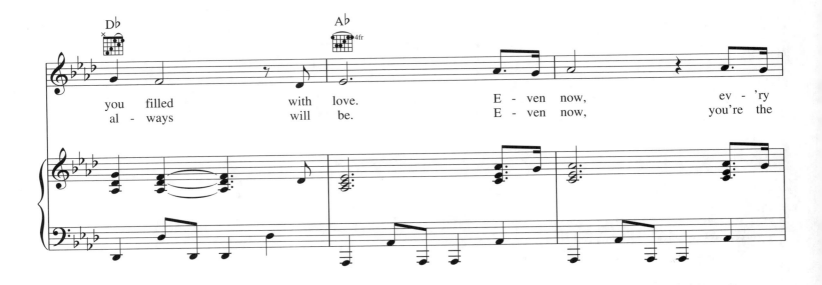

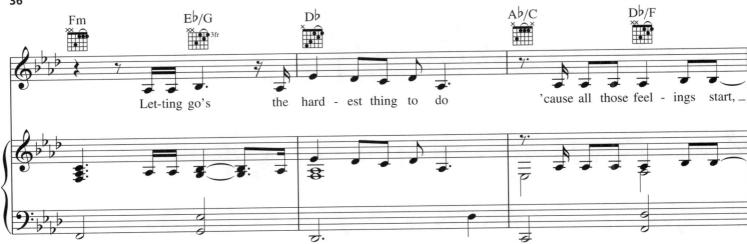

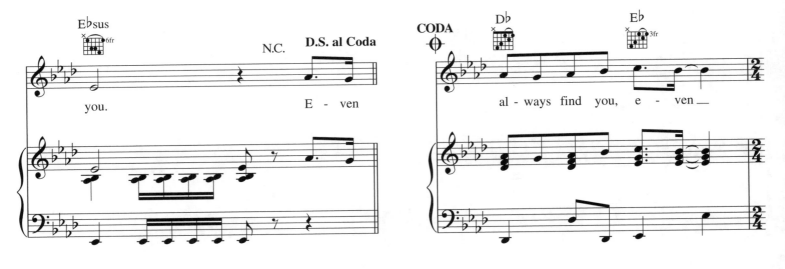

dreams we knew, ___ the rush ___ of you ___ will al-ways ___ be a

part of me. _____

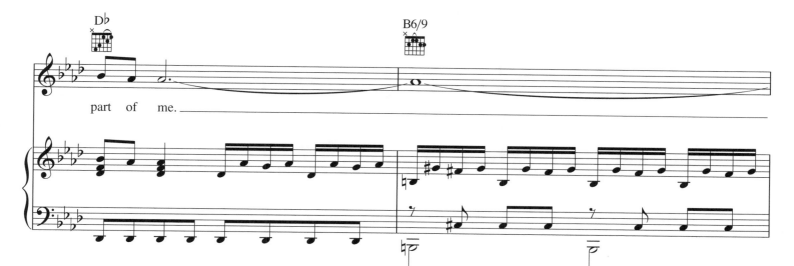

___ E - ven now, you are in my dreams, and in my dreams you

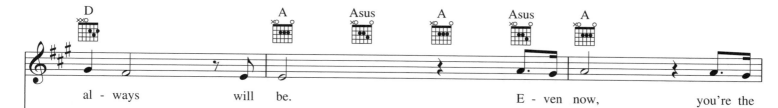

al - ways will be. E - ven now, you're the

one true thing that brings my heart back home here to _____ me. E - ven

now, in my dark - est night, ___ still you shine sil - ver

light. _____ So I fall through for - ev - er with you, e - ven ___

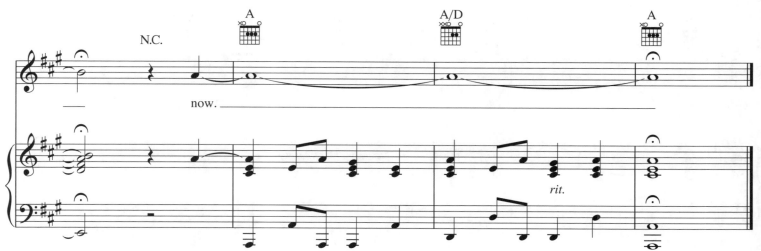

now. _____

EVERYTHING I OWN

Words and Music by
DAVID GATES

Moderately, in 2

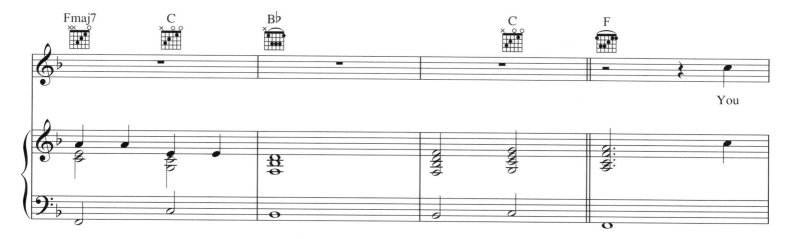

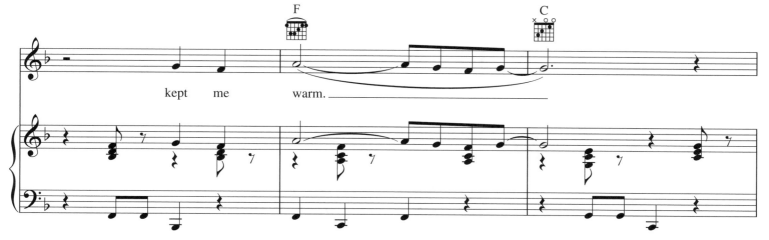

You gave my life to me,

set me free, set me

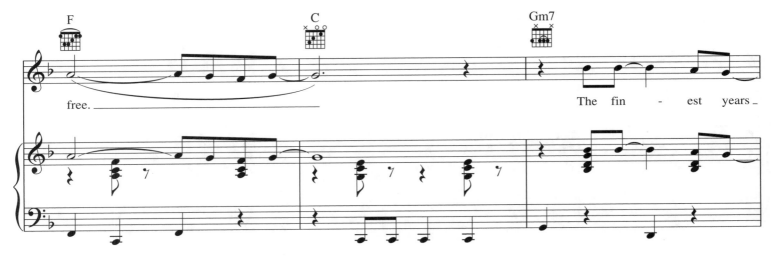

free. The fin - est years

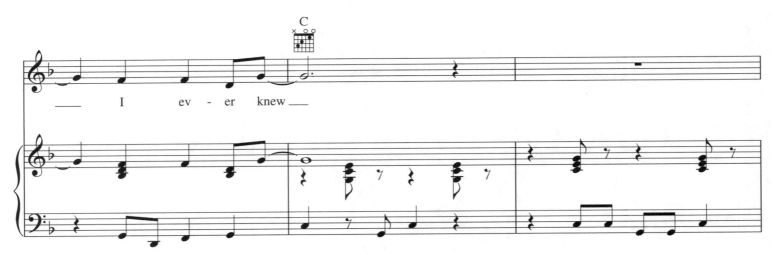

I ev - er knew

is all ___ the years ___ I had with you. And

I would give an - y - thing ___ I own, _

___ give up my life, ___ my heart, _

___ my own. ___ And I would give an -

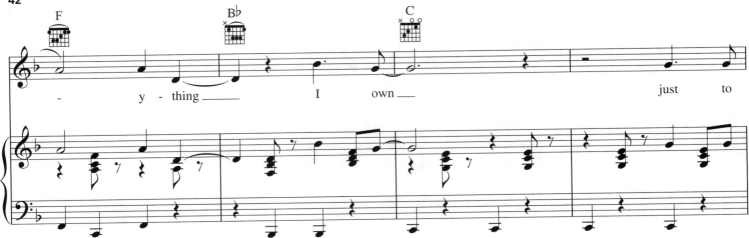

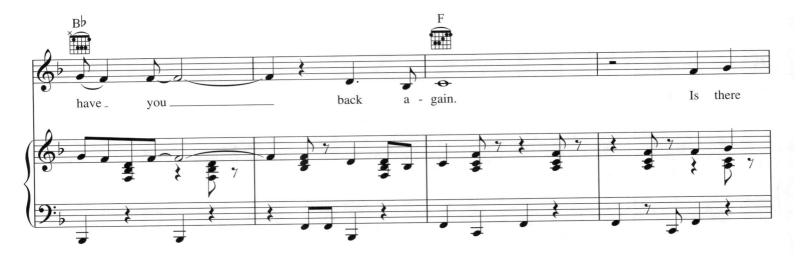

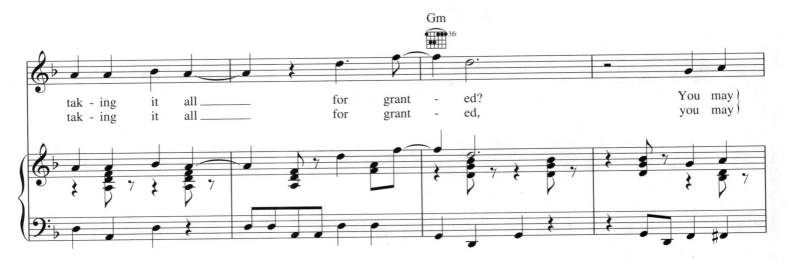

lose them one day; _____ some - one takes them a - way _____ and you

don't hear a word they say. And

C7   F   B♭   C

I would give an - y - thing _____ I own, __

C7   F   B♭   C

give up my life, __ my heart, __ my own. __ And

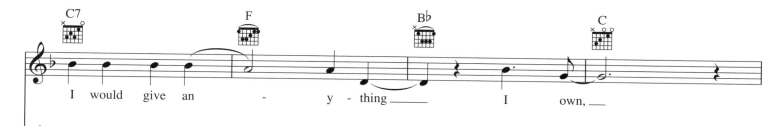

I would give an-y-thing _____ I own ____

____ just to have ___ you _____

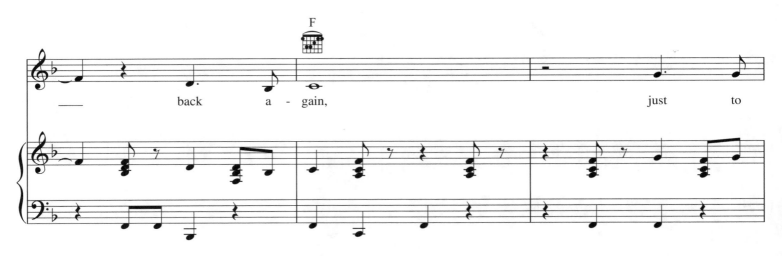

____ back a - gain, just to

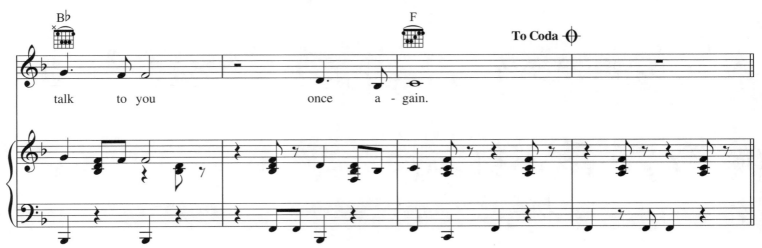

talk to you once a - gain.

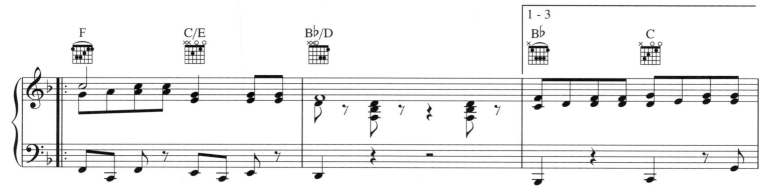

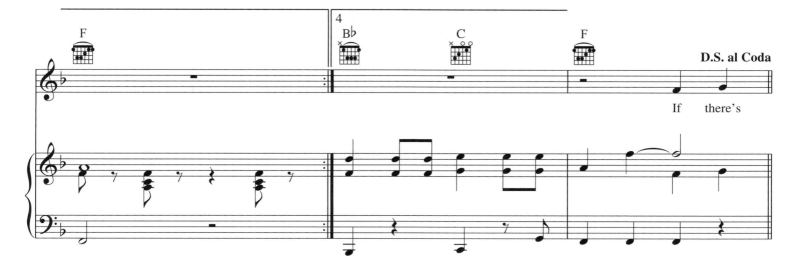

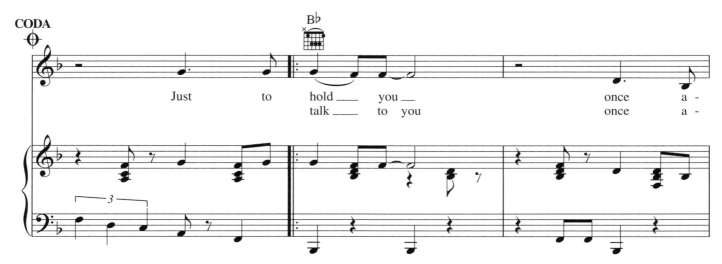

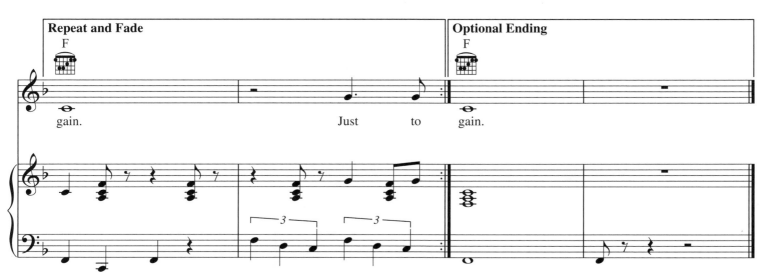

GOODBYE

Words and Music by
PATTY GRIFFIN

Country Rock

Oc - cured   to   me ___
And   I   re - mem - ber   where   I   was ___
To - day   my   heart ___
'Cause   you   can't   make ___

___ the   oth - er   day, ___
- ber   where   I   was ___
___ is   big   and   sore; ___
___ some - bod - y   see ___

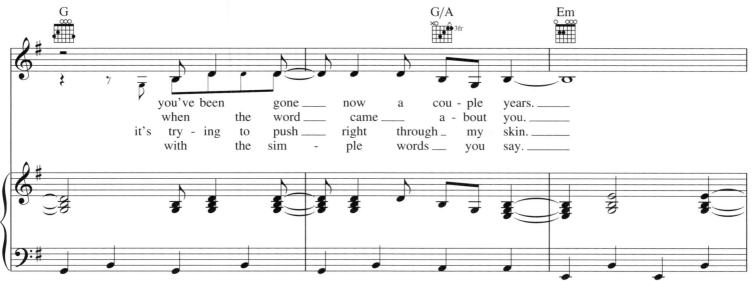

you've been gone ___ now a cou - ple years. ___
when the word ___ came ___ a - bout you. ___
it's try - ing to push ___ right through ___ my skin. ___
with the sim - ple words ___ you say. ___

Well, I guess ___ it takes ___ a while ___
It was a day much like ___ to - day; ___
I won't see ___ you an - y - more; ___
All their beau - ty from ___ with - in, ___

___ for some - one ___ to real -
___ the sky ___ was bright ___
___ I guess that's fi -
___ some - times they ___

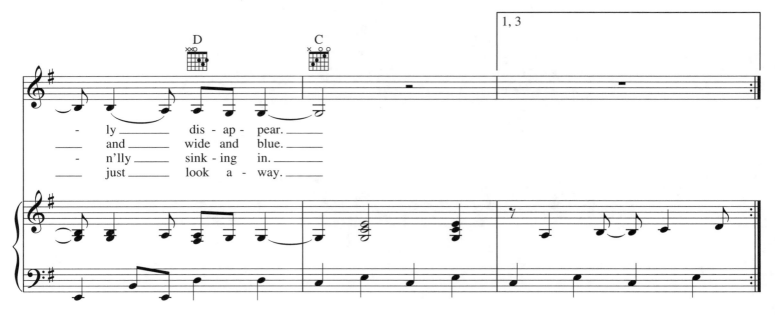

- ly _____ dis-ap- pear. _____
_____ and _____ wide and blue. _____
- n'lly _____ sink-ing in. _____
_____ just _____ look a - way. _____

1, 3

2, 4

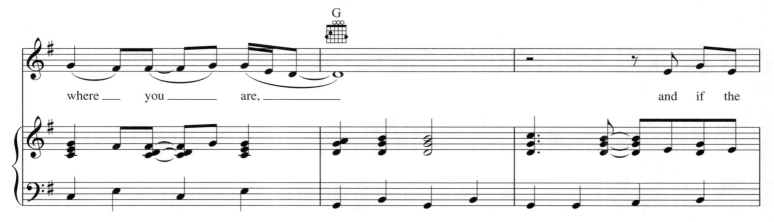

And I won - der _____

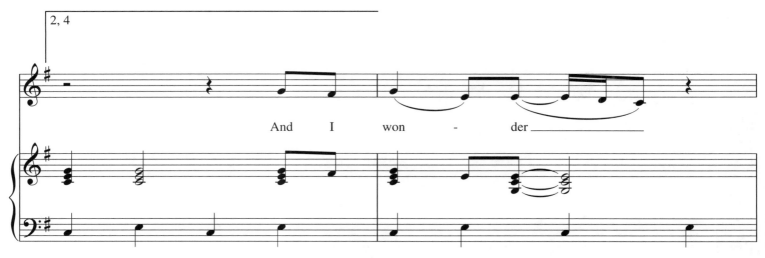

where _____ you _____ are, _____ and if the

pain _____ ends _____ when you _____ die. _____

And I won - der _____ if there _____ was _____

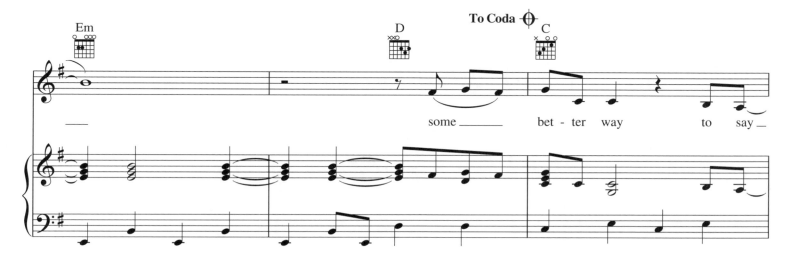

To Coda ⊕

some _____ bet - ter way _____ to say _____

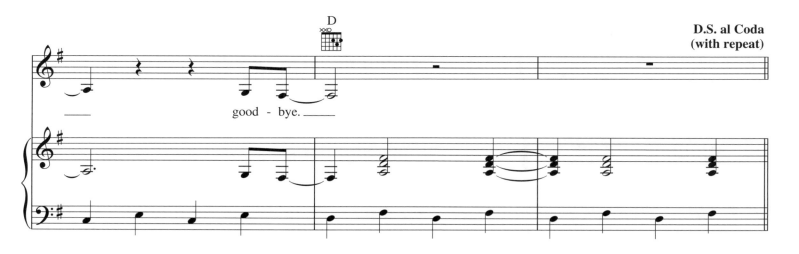

D.S. al Coda
(with repeat)

good - bye. _____

CODA ⊕

bet - ter way _____ to say _____ good - bye, _____

some _____ bet - ter way _____ to say _____ good - bye. _____

Ah. _____ Ah. _____

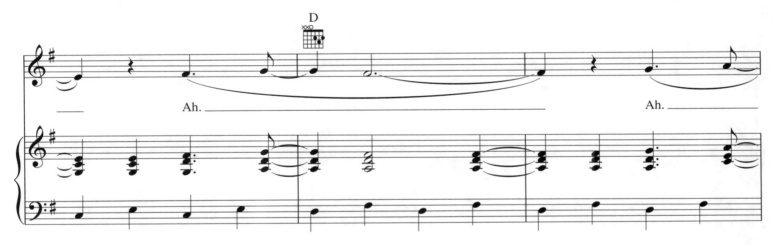

Ah. _____

Ah.

Repeat and Fade

Optional Ending
G

GOODBYE MY FRIEND

Words and Music by
KARLA BONOFF

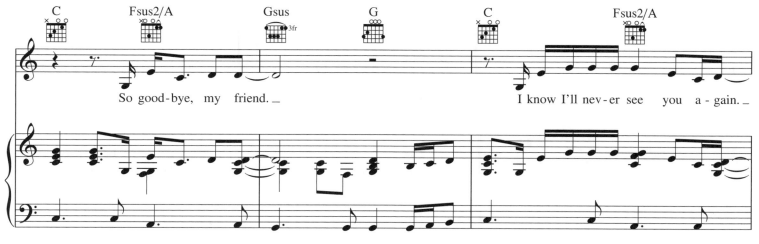

So good-bye, my friend. _ I know I'll nev-er see you a-gain. _

But the time to-geth - er thru all _ the years _ will take a-way _ these _ tears. _ It's o-
But the love you gave _ me thru all _ the years _ will take a-way _ my _ tears. _ I'm o-

kay now. _____ Good - bye, _ my friend.
kay now. _____ Good - bye, _ my

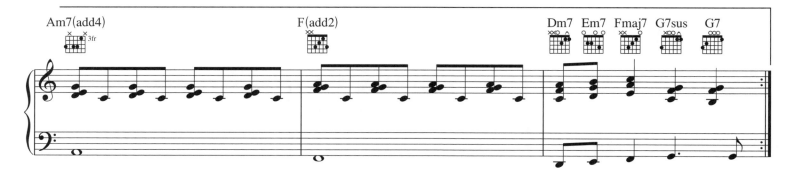

FLY

Words and Music by JEAN JACQUES GOLDMAN,
PHIL GALDSTON and ROLAND ROMANELLI

Slowly, with much freedom

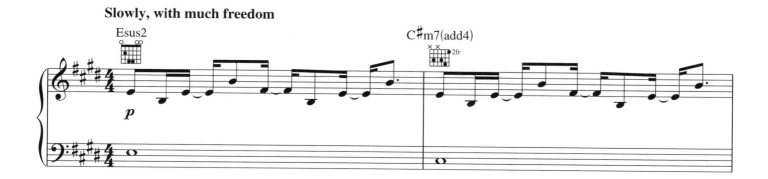

Fly, fly, ___ lit - tle wing,

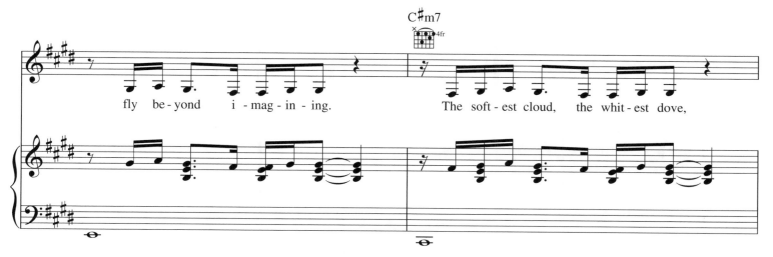

fly be - yond i - mag - in - ing. The soft - est cloud, the whit - est dove,

up - on the wind of heav - en's love. Past ___ the plan - ets ___ and the stars, ___

leave ___ this lone - ly world of ours. Es - cape the sor - row and the pain, ___

and fly a - gain. ___ Fly, fly, ___ pre - cious one,

your end - less ___ jour - ney has be - gun. Take your gen - tle hap - pi - ness,

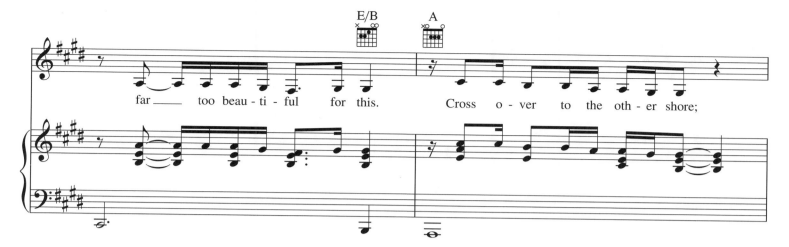

far ____ too beau - ti - ful for this. Cross o - ver to the oth - er shore;

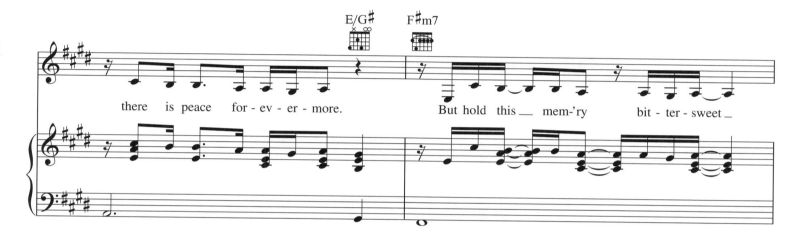

there is peace for - ev - er - more. But hold this ____ mem'ry bit - ter - sweet ____

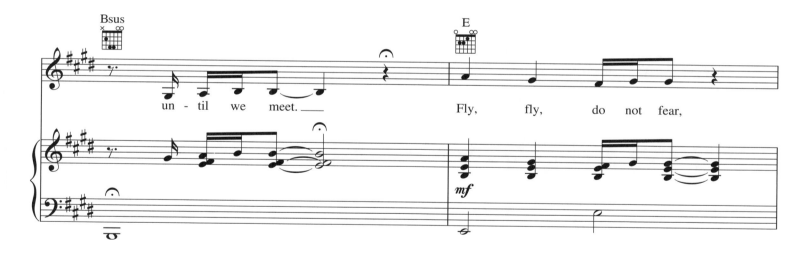

un - til we meet. ____ Fly, fly, do not fear,

don't waste a breath, don't shed a tear. Your heart is pure, your soul is free.

Be on your way; don't wait for me. __ A - bove __ the u - ni - verse you'll climb,

on be - yond the hands of time. __ The moon will rise, the sun will set, __

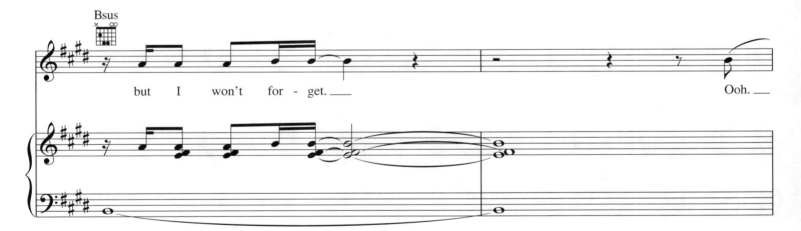

but I won't for - get. __ Ooh. __

Ooh. __

Ooh.

Ah.

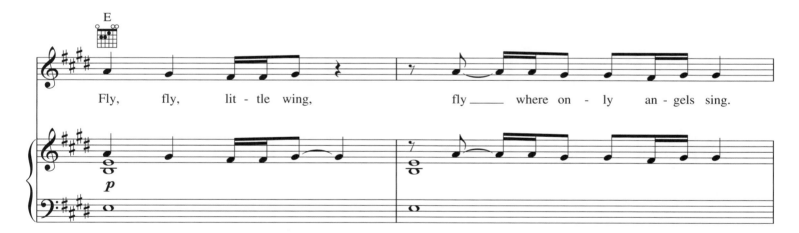

Fly, fly, lit - tle wing, fly _____ where on - ly an - gels sing.

Fly a - way; the time is right. Go now, _ find the light. _

HOLES IN THE FLOOR OF HEAVEN

Words and Music by WILLIAM A. KIRSCH
and STEVE WARINER

Recorded a half step lower.

How I cried_ when the sky let go_ with a cold and lone-some rain._
Year by year_____ we made a life_ in this sleep - y lit - tle town. __
They throw the rice, _ I catch her eye_ as the rain starts com - ing down. __

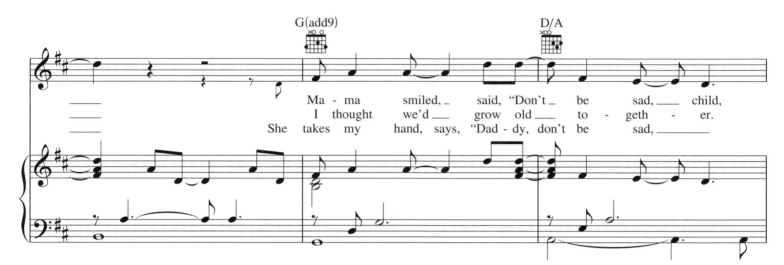

_____ Ma - ma smiled, _ said, "Don't_ be sad, _ child,
_____ I thought we'd_ grow old_ to - geth - er.
_____ She takes my hand, says, "Dad - dy, don't be sad, _____

Grand - ma's watch - ing you_ to - day." _____
Lord, I sure do miss_ her now. _____
'cause I know Ma - ma's watch - ing now." _____

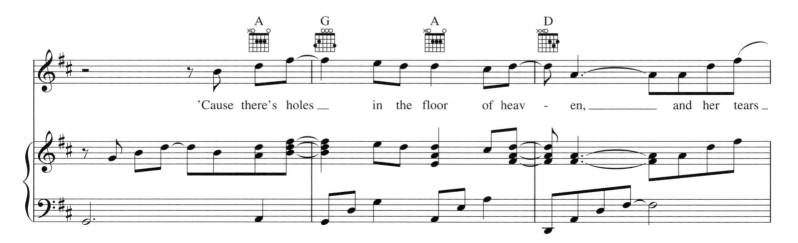

'Cause there's holes_ in the floor of heav - en, _____ and her tears_

are pour - ing down. That's how { you / I } know __ she's watch -

- ing, wish - ing she could be here now. __ And

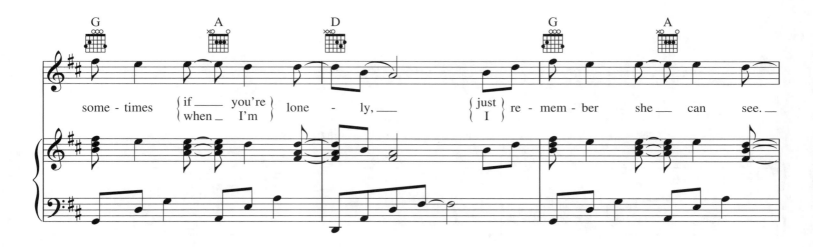

some - times { if __ you're / when __ I'm } lone - ly, __ { just / I } re - mem - ber she __ can see.

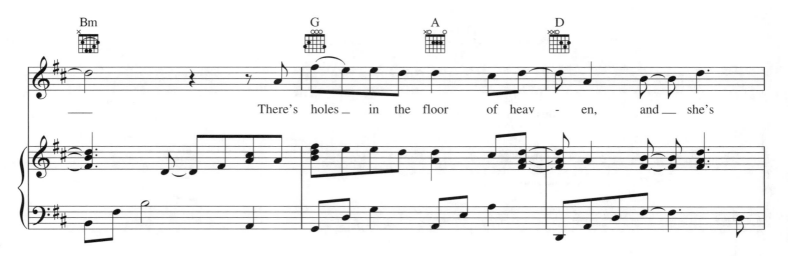

__ There's holes __ in the floor of heav - en, and __ she's

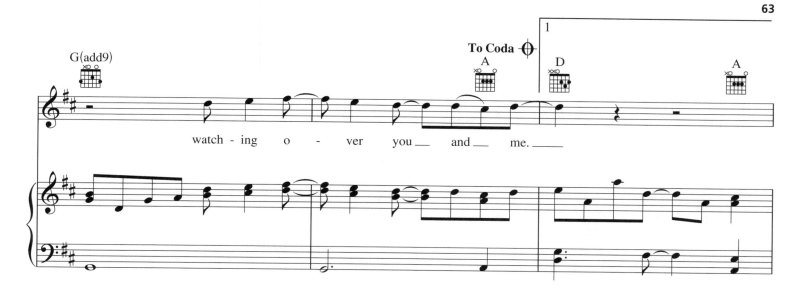

watch - ing o - ver you ___ and ___ me. ___

Well,   my

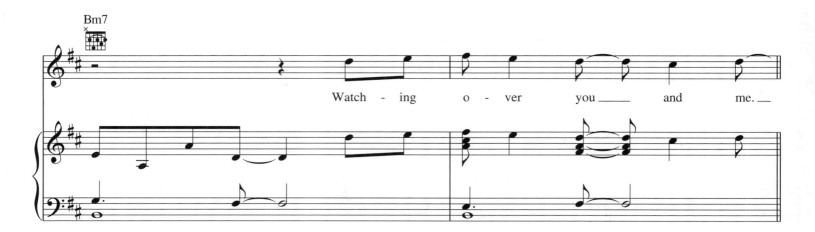

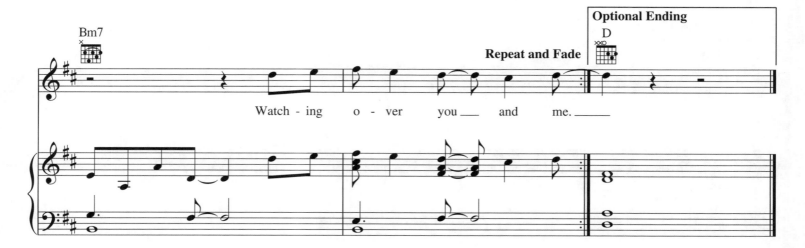

HERE WITHOUT YOU

Words and Music by MATT ROBERTS, BRAD ARNOLD,
CHRISTOPHER HENDERSON and ROBERT HARRELL

Moderate Rock

A hun-dred days have made me old-er since the last time that I saw your pret-ty face. A thou-sand

* Recorded a half step lower.

lies have made me cold - er and I don't think I can look at this the same.

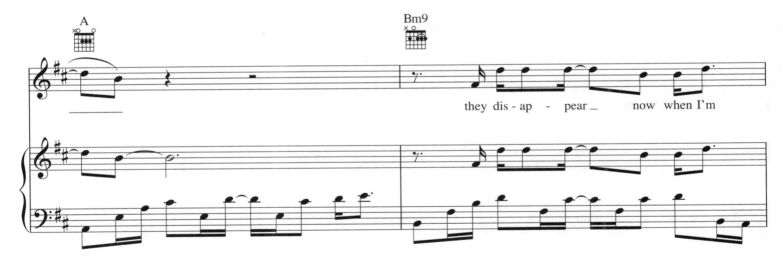

But all the miles that sep-ar-ate,

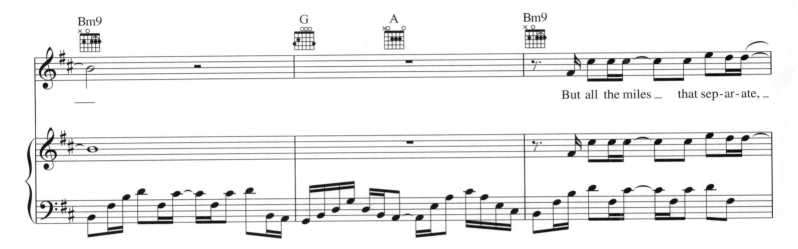

they dis - ap - pear now when I'm

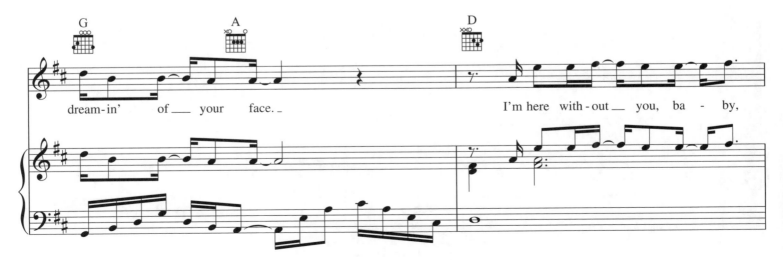

dream-in' of your face. I'm here with-out you, ba - by,

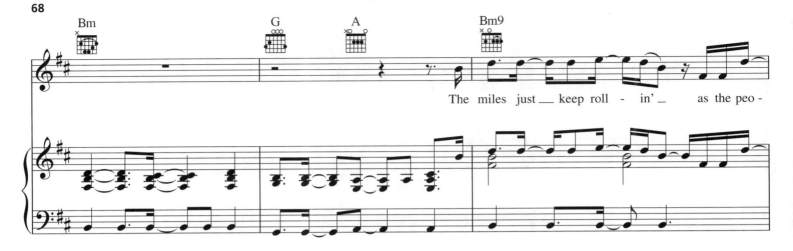

The miles just __ keep roll - in' __ as the peo -

- ple leave __ their way __ to say __ hel - lo. __

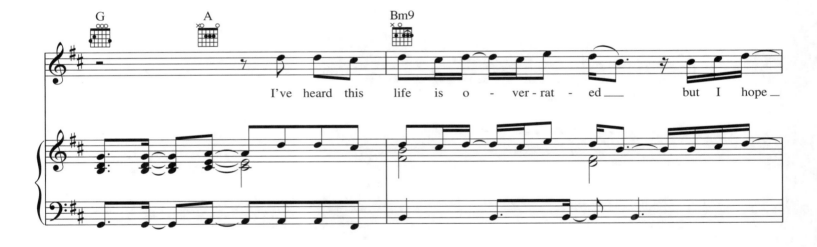

I've heard this life is o - ver - rat - ed __ but I hope __

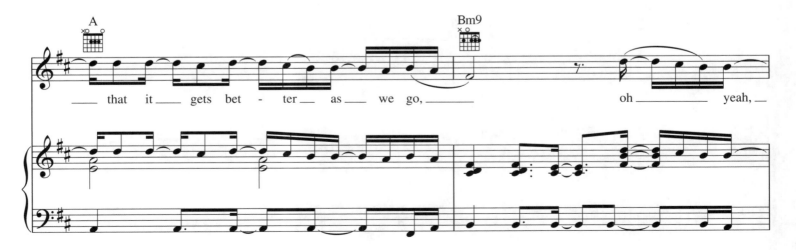

__ that it __ gets bet - ter as __ we go, __ oh __ yeah, __

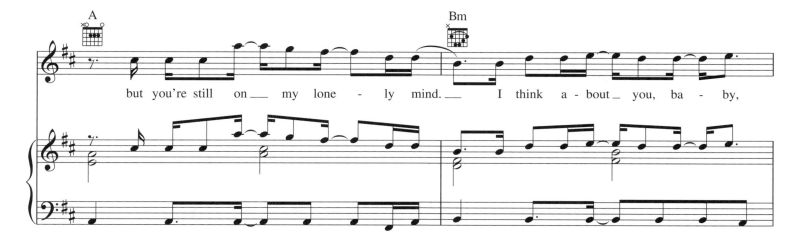

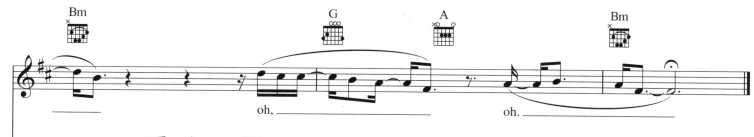

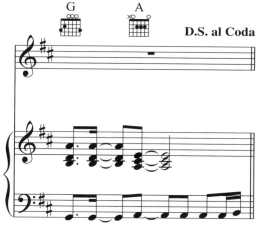

I BELIEVE

Words and Music by SKIP EWING
and DONNY KEES

Slowly, with feeling

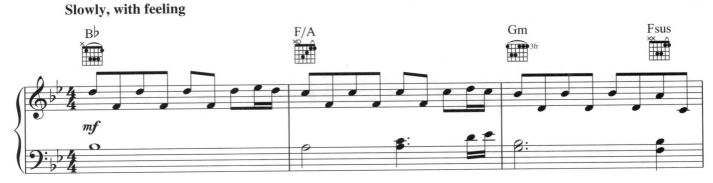

Ev -'ry now __ and then, soft as breath __ up-on __ my skin, __ I feel __

__ you come back a-gain and it's like you have-n't been __ gone a mo-

-ment from __ my side. __ Like the tears __ were nev-er cried. Like the hands __

of time ___ are hold - ing you ___ and me. ___ And with

all my heart ___ I'm sure we're clos - er than we ev - er were. I don't ___ have ___

___ to hear ___ or see. I've got ___ all ___ the proof ___ I need. There ___ are more ___

___ than an - gels watch-ing o - ver me, ___ I be - lieve. ___

Oh, I be - lieve. ___ Now when you

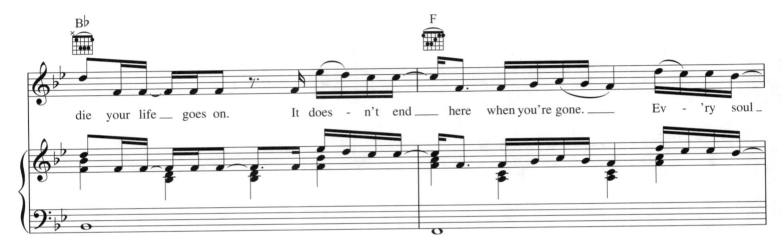

die your life ___ goes on. It does - n't end ___ here when you're gone. ___ Ev - 'ry soul ___

___ is filled ___ with light. It nev - er ends, ___ if I'm right. Our ___ love can

e - ven reach ___ a - cross ___ e - ter - ni - ty, _____ I be - lieve. ___

Oh, I be - lieve. ____

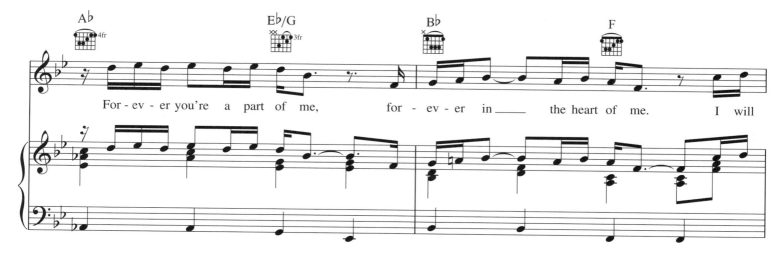

For - ev - er you're a part of me, for - ev - er in ____ the heart of me. I will

hold you e - ven long - er if I can. _____ Oh, the

peo - ple who ____ don't see the most see that I ____ be - lieve in ghosts.

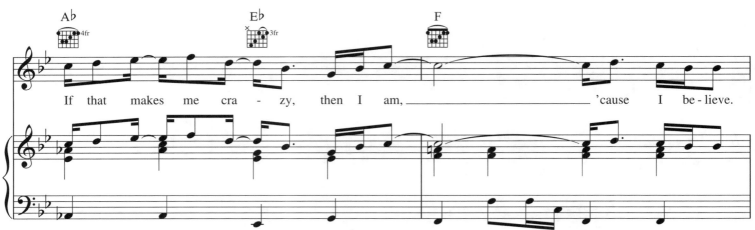

If that makes me cra - zy, then I am, _____ 'cause I be - lieve.

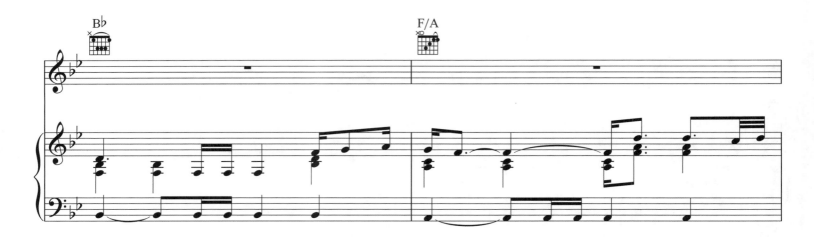

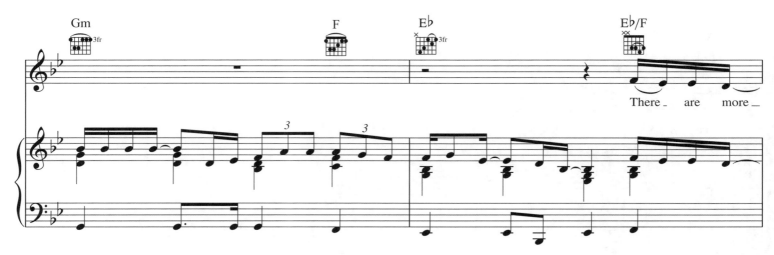

There _ are more _

_ than an - gels watch - ing o - ver me _____ I be - lieve. _

Oh, I be - lieve. ___

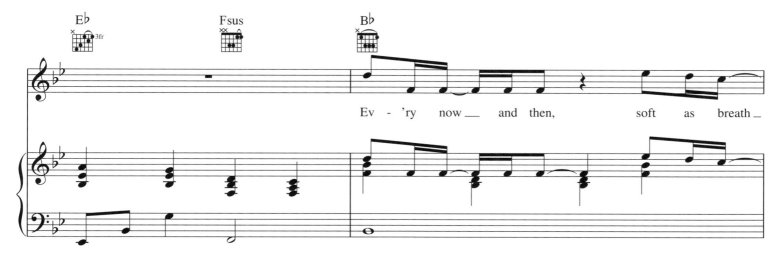

Ev - 'ry now ___ and then, ___ soft as breath ___

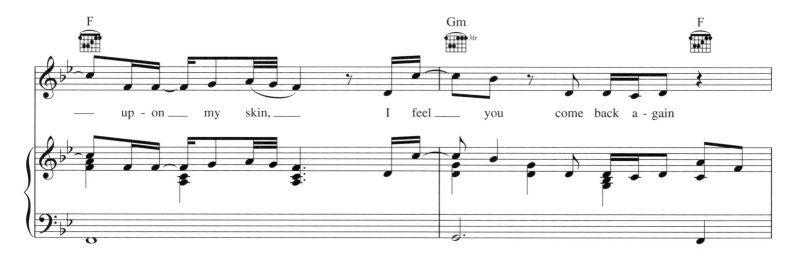

___ up - on ___ my skin, ___ I feel ___ you come back a - gain

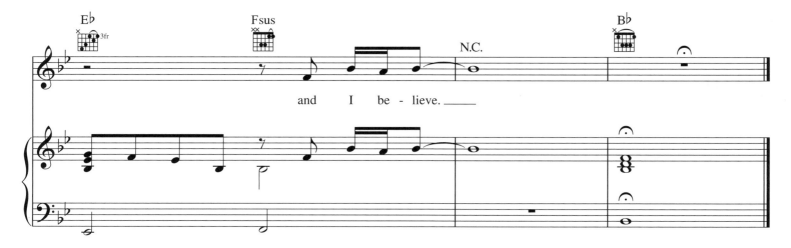

and I be - lieve. _____

I MISS MY FRIEND

Words and Music by TOM SHAPIRO,
TONY MARTIN and MARK NESLER

Moderately

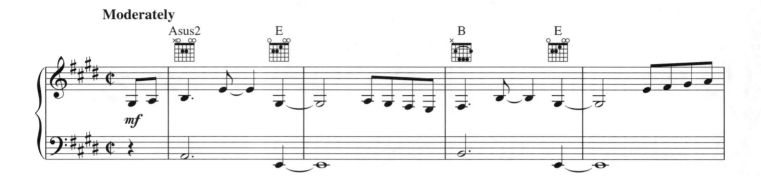

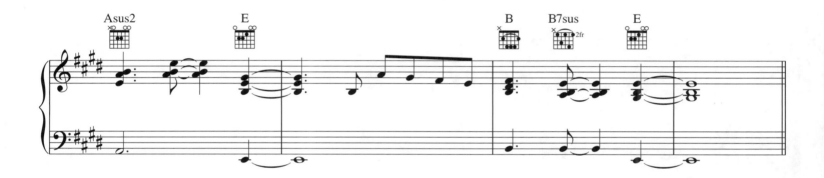

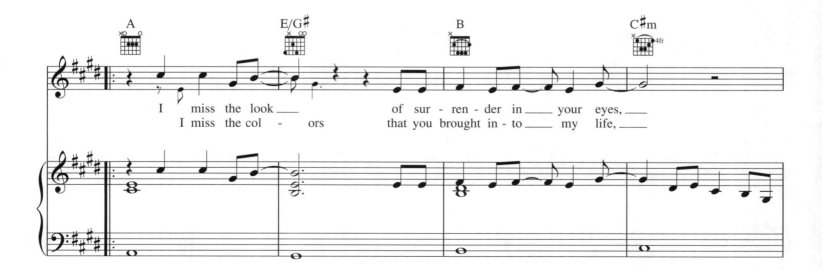

I miss the look ___ of sur - ren - der in ___ your eyes, ___

I miss the col - ors ___ that you brought in - to ___ my life, ___

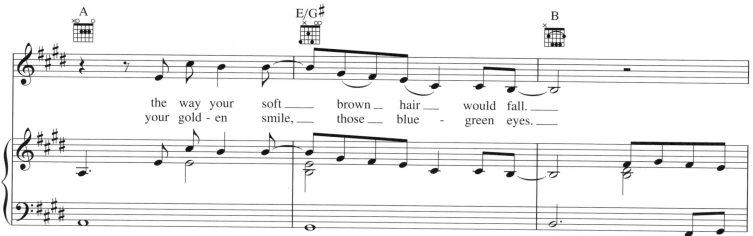

the way your soft ___ brown ___ hair ___ would fall. ___
your gold - en smile, ___ those ___ blue - green eyes. ___

And I miss ___ your gen - tle voice
I miss the pow - er of your

in lone - ly times like now, ___
kiss when we ___ made ___ love. ___

Oh, but ba - by, most ___ of all, ___
say - in' it - 'll be ___ al - right. ___

I miss ___ my friend. ___

The

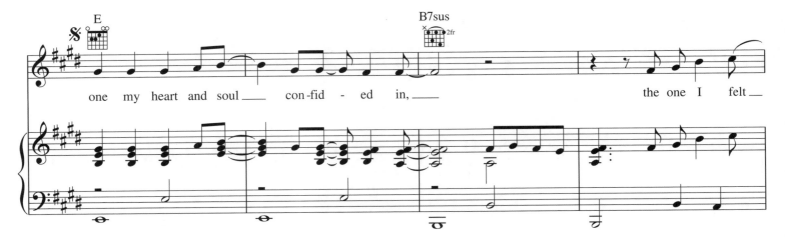

one my heart and soul __ con-fid - ed in, __ the one I felt __

__ the saf - est with. __ The one who knew __ just what to say __

to make me laugh a - gain __ and let the light back

To Coda

in. __ I miss __ my friend. __

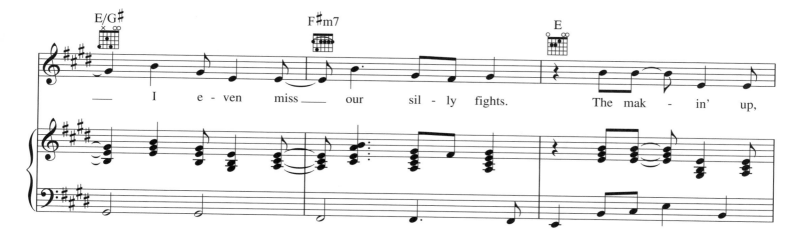

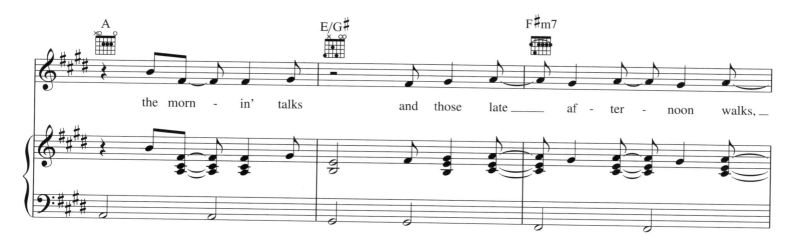

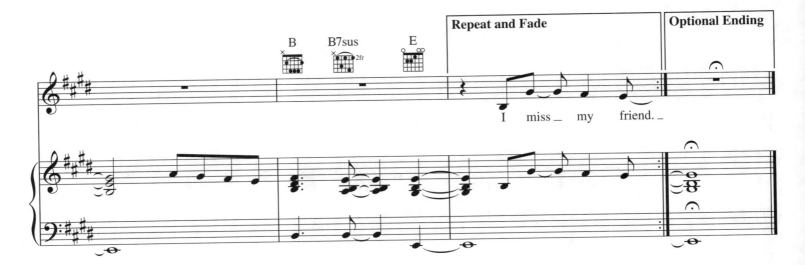

I WILL REMEMBER YOU
Theme from THE BROTHERS McMULLEN

Words and Music by SARAH McLACHLAN,
SEAMUS EGAN and DAVE MERENDA

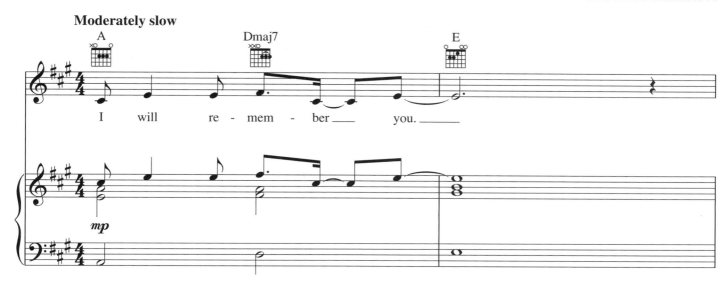

Moderately slow

I will re - mem - ber ____ you. ____

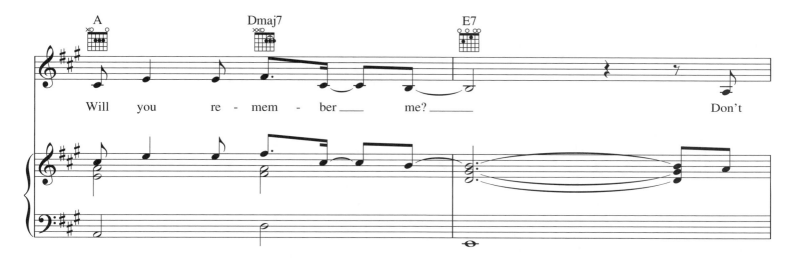

Will you re - mem - ber ____ me? ____ Don't

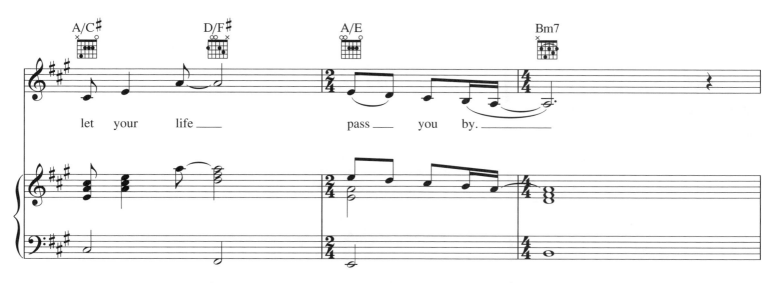

let your life ____ pass ____ you by. ____

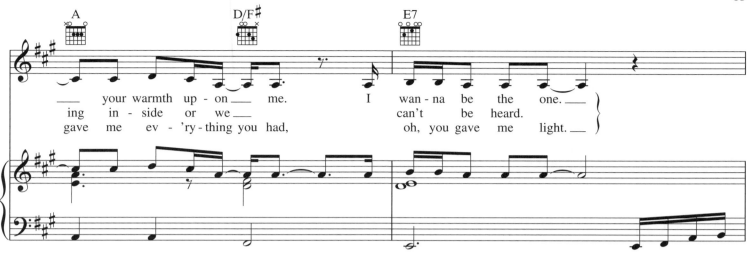

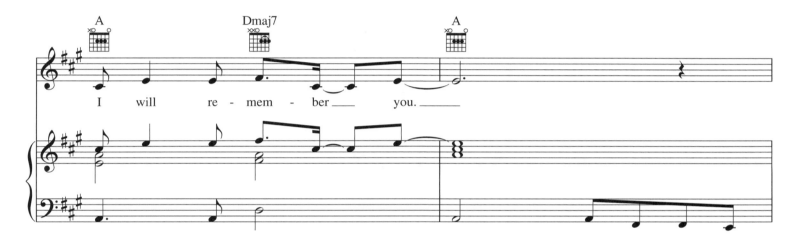

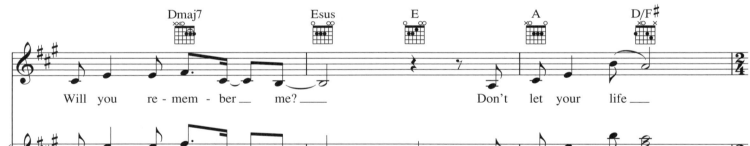

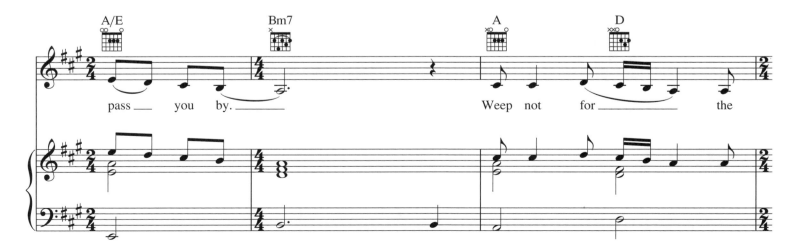

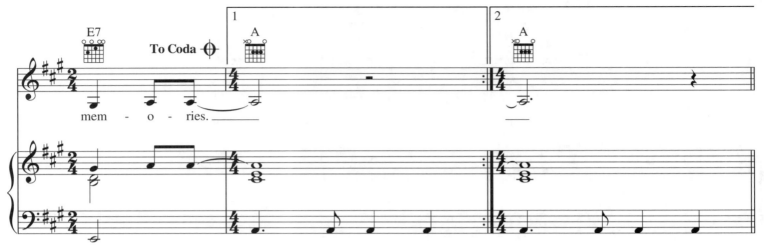

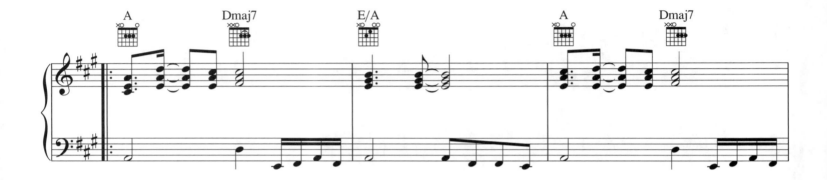

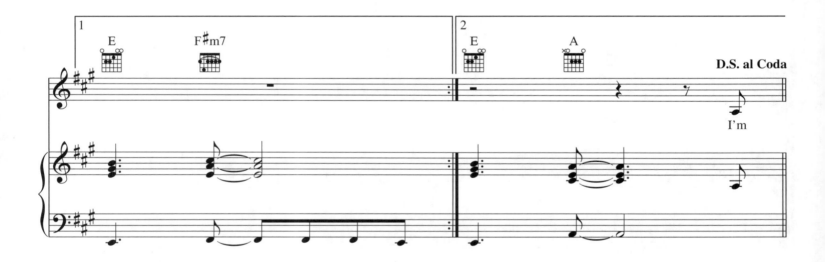

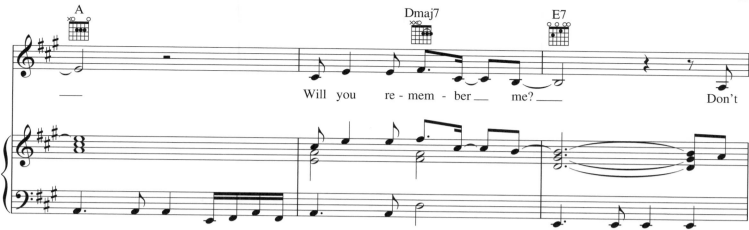

Will you re-mem-ber ___ me? ___ Don't

let your life ___ pass ___ you by. ___

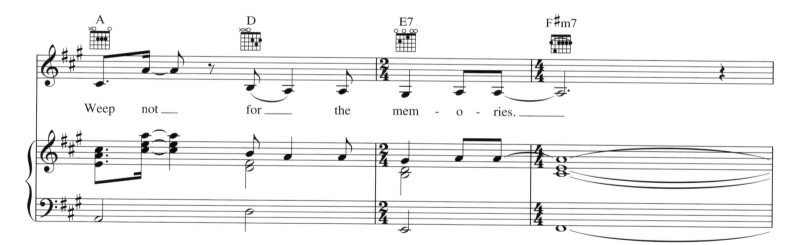

Weep not ___ for ___ the mem-o-ries. ___

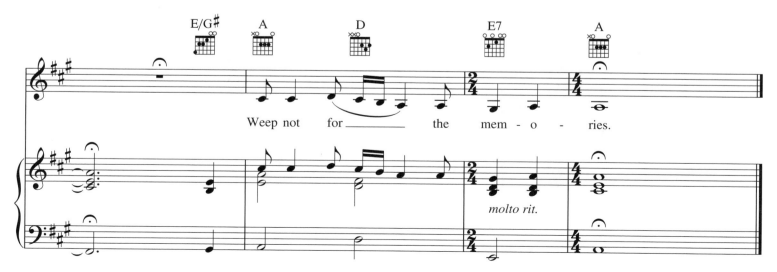

Weep not for ___ the mem-o-ries.

molto rit.

I WOULD'VE LOVED YOU ANYWAY

Words and Music by MARY DANNA
and TROY VERGES

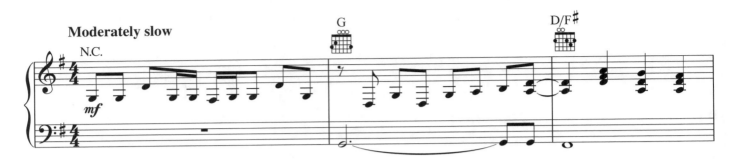

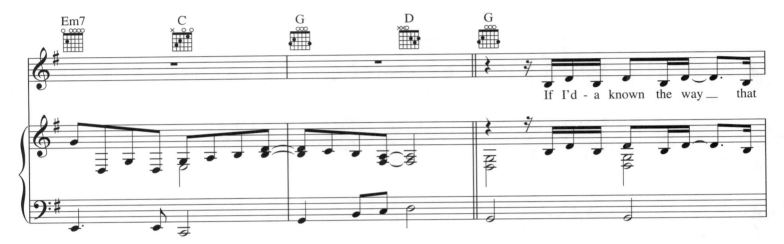

hurt, I would-'ve loved you an - y - way. _____ I'd do it all the same, _

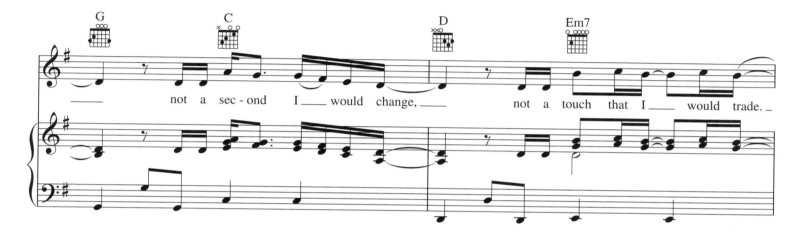

_ not a sec - ond I _ would change, ____ not a touch that I ___ would trade. _

_____ Had _ I known my heart would _ break, I'd have loved you an - y -

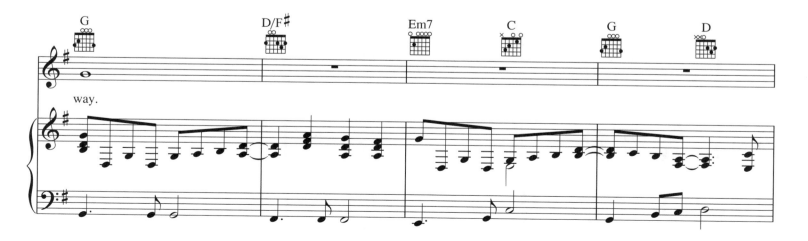

way.

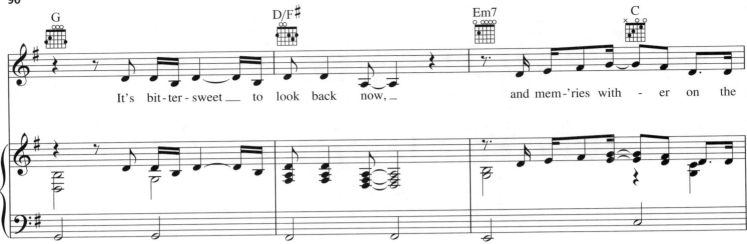

It's bit-ter-sweet ___ to look back now, ___ and mem-'ries with - er on the

vine. But just to hold ___ you close to me, ___

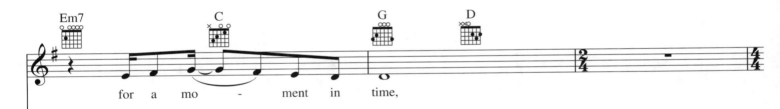

for a mo - ment in time,

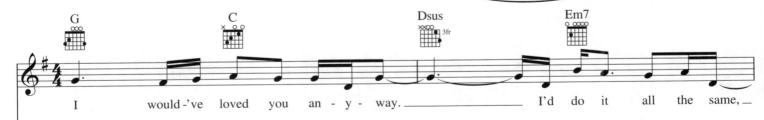

I would-'ve loved you an-y-way. ___ I'd do it all the same, ___

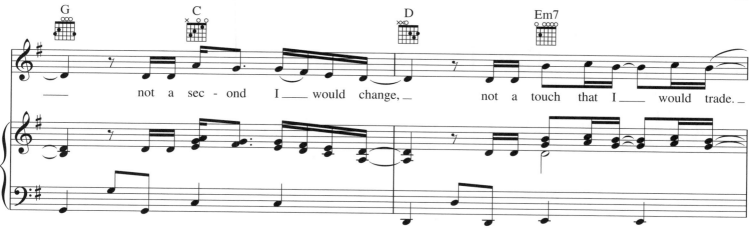

not a sec-ond I____ would change,____ not a touch that I____ would trade.____

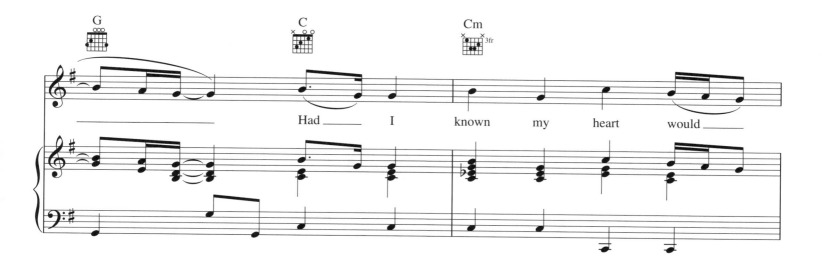

____ Had ____ I known my heart would ____

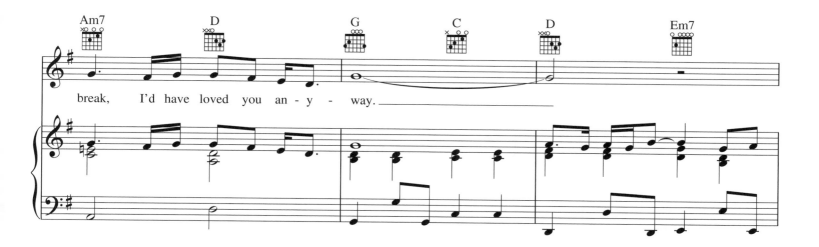

break, I'd have loved you an-y-way. _____

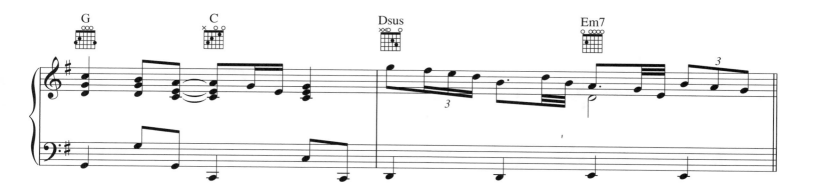

And e - ven if ___ I'd seen it com - in', you'd still - 've seen ___ me

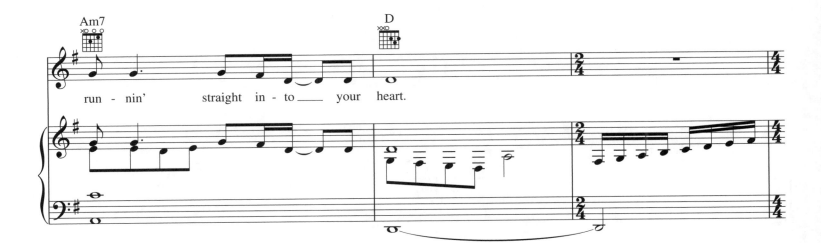

run - nin' straight in - to ___ your heart.

I would-'ve loved you an - y - way. _____ I'd do it all the same, _

not a sec - ond I ___ would change, _ not a touch that I ___ would trade. _

Had ___ I known my heart would ___ break,

I would-'ve loved you an - y - way. ___

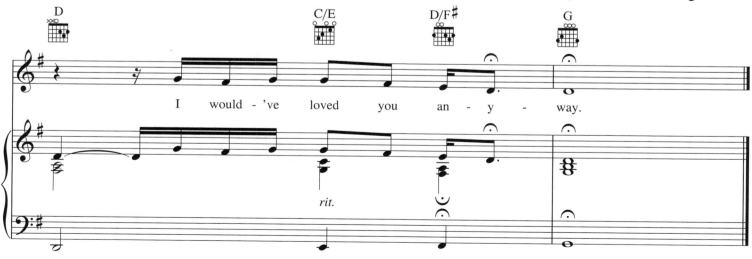

I would - 've loved you an - y - way.

rit.

IF I COULD BE WHERE YOU ARE

Words by ROMA RYAN
Music by ENYA and NICKY RYAN

Slowly, with much freedom

Where _ are _ you this _ mo - ment?
I'm _ lost _ now with - out you. I

On - ly in my dreams. _ You're _ miss - ing, _ but you're _
don't _ know where you are. _ I keep watch - ing, _ I keep _

al - ways a heart - beat from ___ me. ___
hop - ing, but time ___ keeps us ___ a - part.

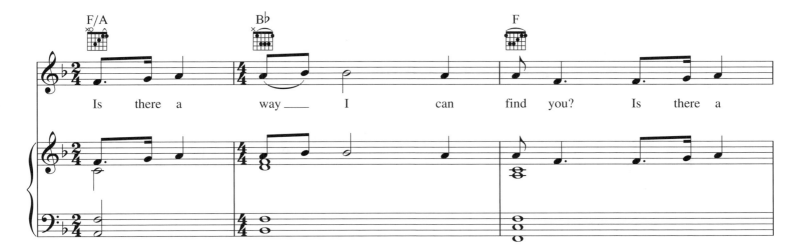

Is there a way ___ I can find you? Is there a

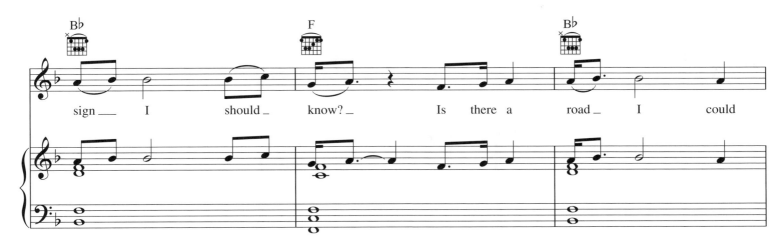

sign ___ I should ___ know? ___ Is there a road ___ I could

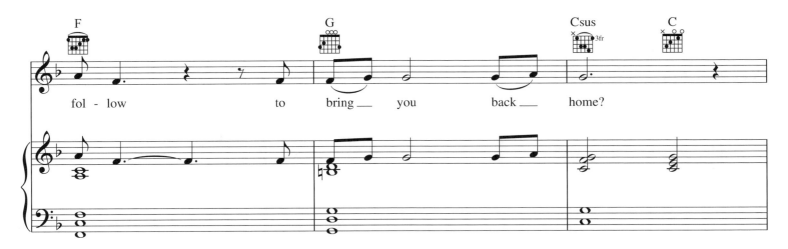

fol - low to bring ___ you back ___ home?

Win - ter _____ lies be - fore me; now you're _ so far a -

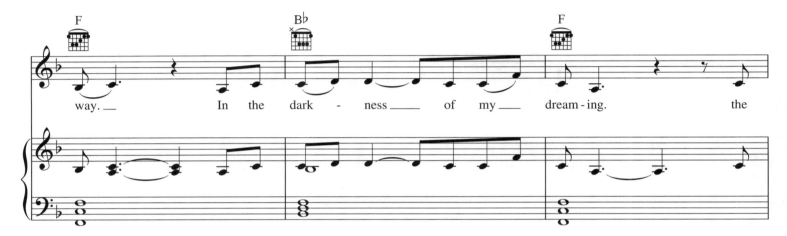

way. _____ In the dark - ness _____ of my _____ dream - ing. the

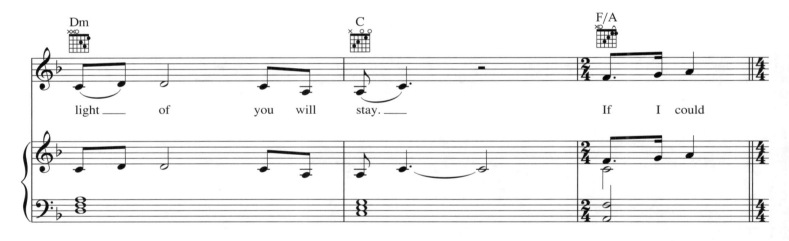

light _____ of you will stay. _____ If I could

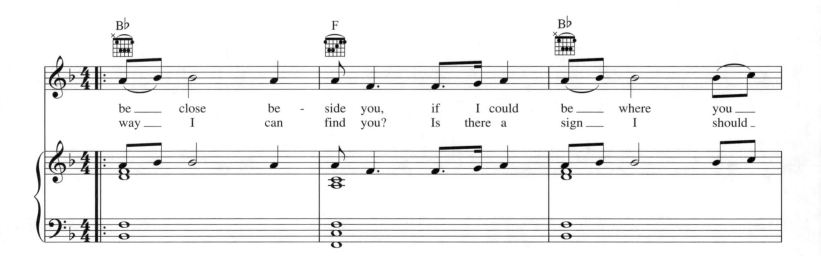

be _____ close be - side you, if I could be _____ where you _____ the
way _____ I can find you? Is there a sign _____ I should _

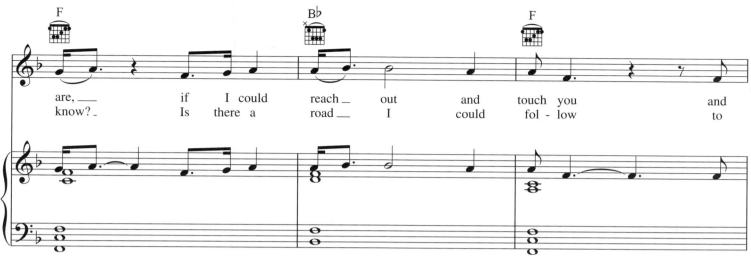

are, ___   if   I   could   reach ___ out   and   touch you   and
know? ___   Is   there a   road ___ I   could   fol - low   to

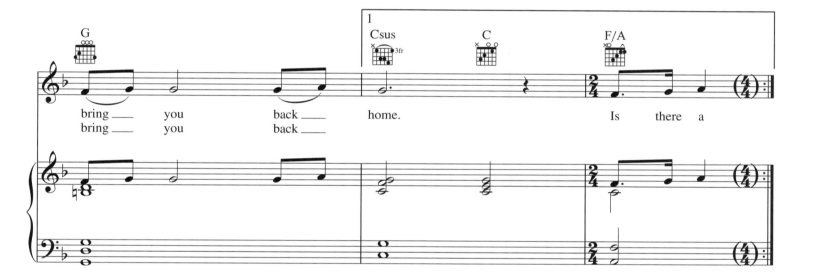

bring ___ you   back ___ home.   Is   there   a
bring ___ you   back ___

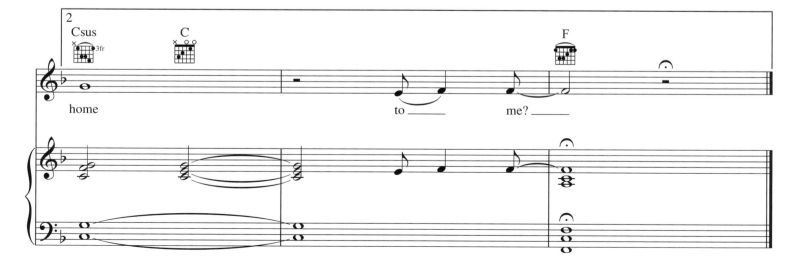

home   to ___ me? ___

IF I HAD ONLY KNOWN

Words and Music by CRAIG MORRIS
and JANA STANFIELD

un - der - neath __ the thun - der we'd be warm.
keep your words __ a - live __ in - side my head.

If

I had on - ly known _____
I had on - ly known _____

it was our last ___ walk in ___ the
I'd nev - er hear ___ your voice __ a -

rain.
gain.

If I had

You were the

treas - ure in ___ my hand. ___ You were the one who al - ways stood __ be - side __ me,

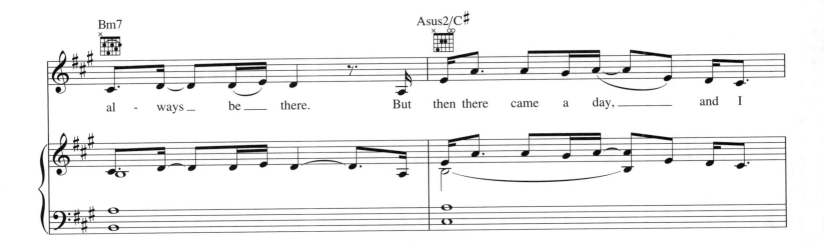

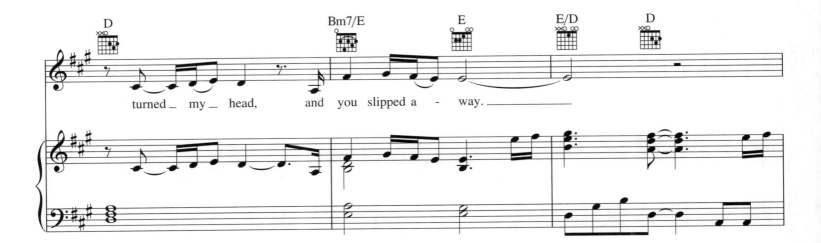

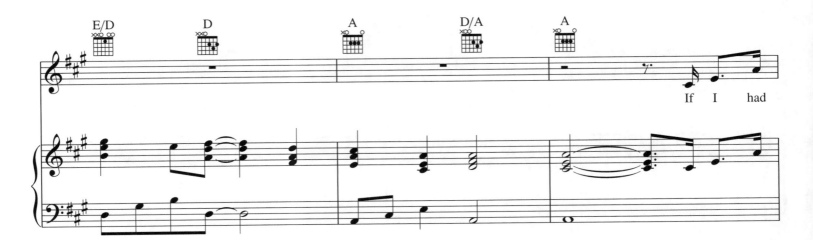

on - ly known __ it was my last night __ by your side, I'd

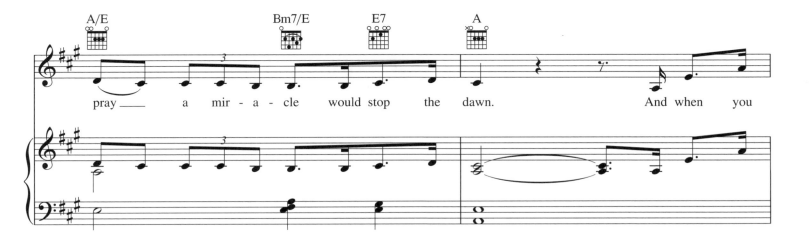

pray ___ a mir - a - cle would stop the dawn. And when you

smiled at me, ____ I would look in - to your eyes __ and make

sure you knew my love for you goes on and on. _____

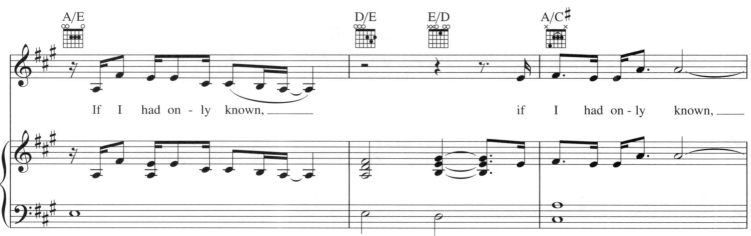

If I had on-ly known, _____ if I had on-ly known, _____

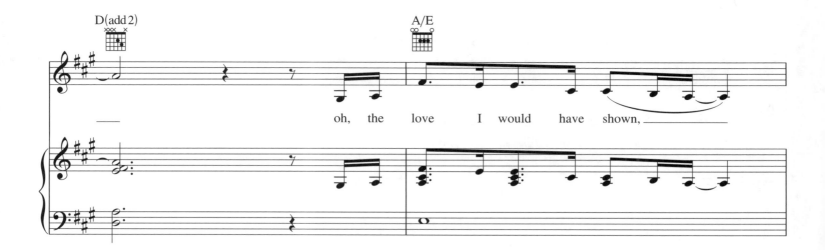

_____ oh, the love I would have shown, _____

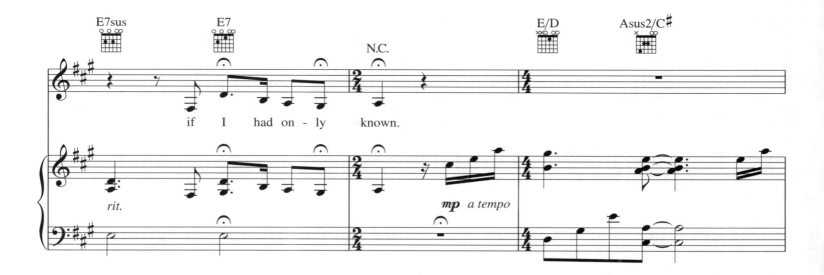

if I had on-ly known.

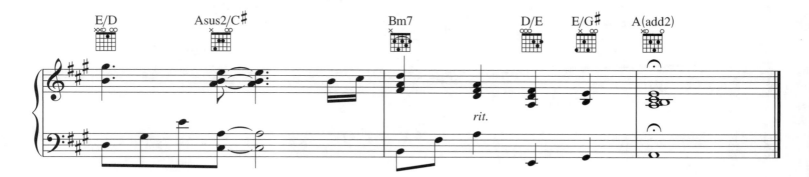

I'M YOUR ANGEL

Words and Music by
ROBERT KELLY

No moun-tain's too high ____ for you to
I saw ____ your tear - drops and I heard you

climb. ____
cry. ____

All ____ you have ____ to do ____ is have ____ some climb-
All ____ you need ____ is time. ____ Seek me and you _

- ing faith, _
____ shall find. _

oh, yeah. ____

No riv-er's too wide ____ for you to
You have ev-'ry-thing ____ and you're still

make it a-cross. All you have to do is be-lieve
lone - ly. It don't have to be this way. Let me show you

it when you pray. And then you will see, the morn-ing will come, and
a bet - ter day. And then you will see, the morn-ing will come, and

ev - er - y day will be bright as the sun. All of your fears, cast them on me.
all of your days will be bright as the sun. So all of your fears, just cast them on me.

I just want you to see. } I'll be your cloud up in the sky, I'll be your
How can I make you see? }

shoul- der when _ you cry. _ I'll hear your _ voic- es when you call _____ me. I am your

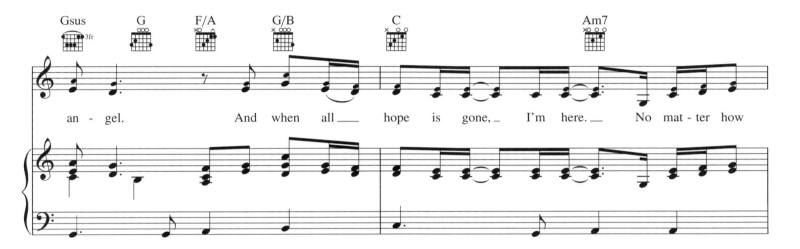

an- gel. And when all ____ hope is gone, _ I'm here. _ No mat- ter how

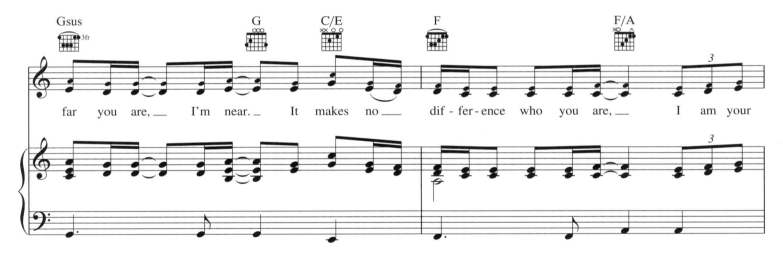

far you are, ____ I'm near. _ It makes no ____ dif- fer- ence who you are, ____ I am your

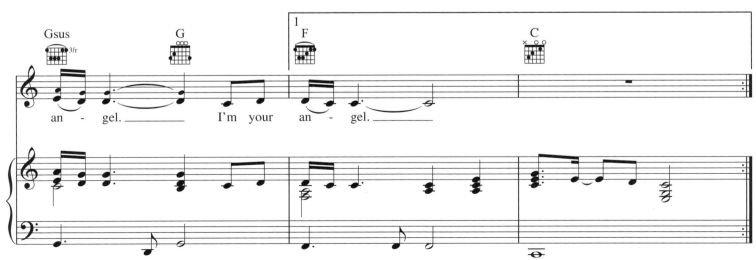

an- gel. _____ I'm your an - gel. _____

an - gel.   And when it's time __ to face __ the storm, __ I'll be right by __ your __

side. Grace will keep __ us safe __ and warm, __   and I know __ we will __ sur - vive. __

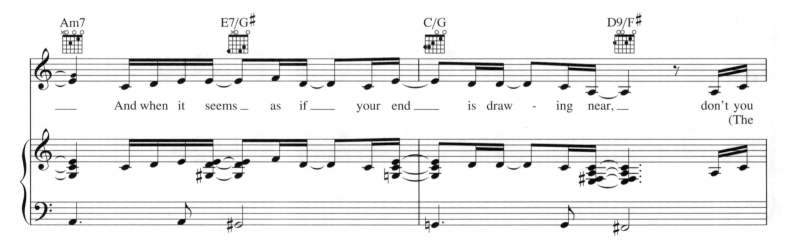

__ And when it seems __ as if __ your end __ is draw - ing near, __   don't you
(The

dare give up __ the fight __   Just put your trust be - yond __ the sky. __   I'll be your
end is draw - ing near.) __

INTO THE WEST

from THE LORD OF THE RINGS: THE RETURN OF THE KING

Words and Music by ANNIE LENNOX,
HOWARD SHORE and FRAN WALSH

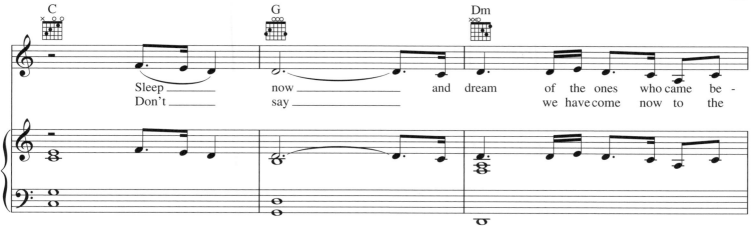

Sleep _____ now _____ and dream of the ones who came be -
Don't _____ say _____ we have come now to the

fore. _____
end. _____

They are call - ing _____
White shores are call - ing. _____

To Coda ⊕

from a-cross a dis - tant shore.
You and I will meet a -

Why do you weep? ___

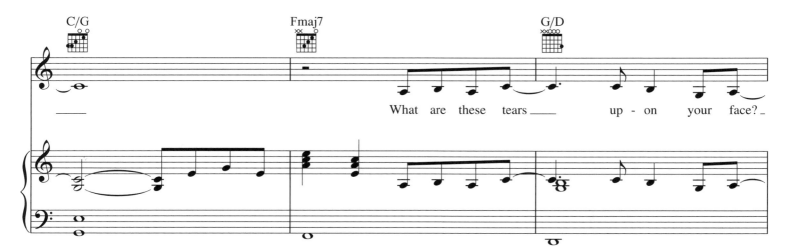

_____ What are these tears _____ up - on your face? ___

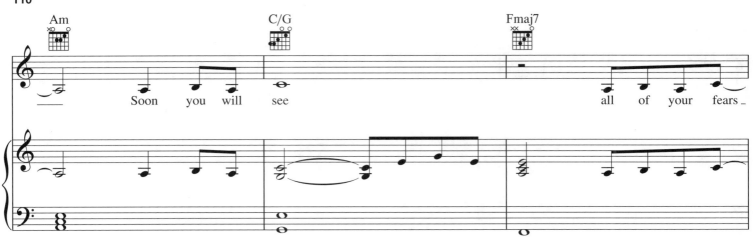

Am   C/G   Fmaj7

Soon you will see all of your fears

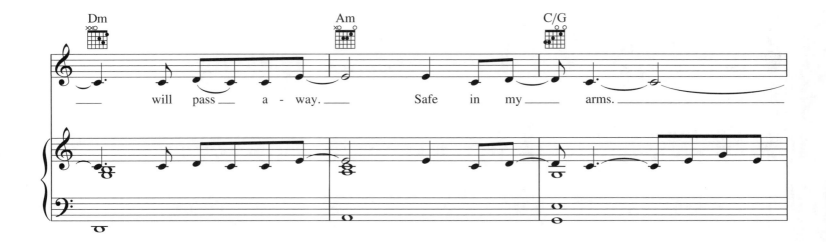

Dm   Am   C/G

will pass a - way. Safe in my arms.

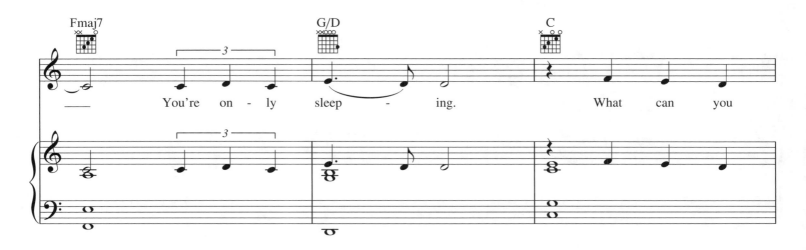

Fmaj7   G/D   C

You're on - ly sleep - ing. What can you

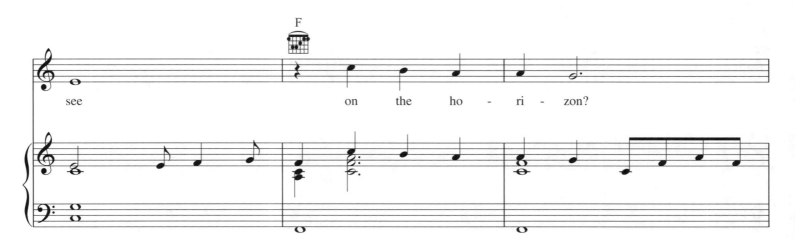

F

see on the ho - ri - zon?

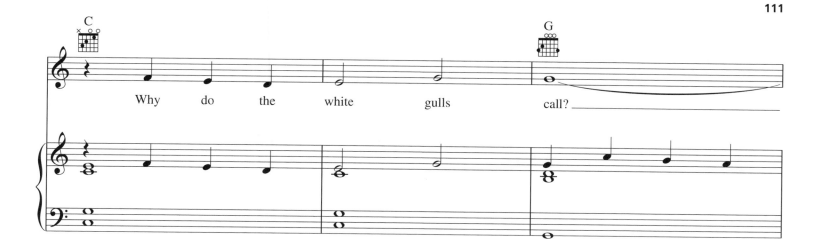

Why do the white gulls call? _____

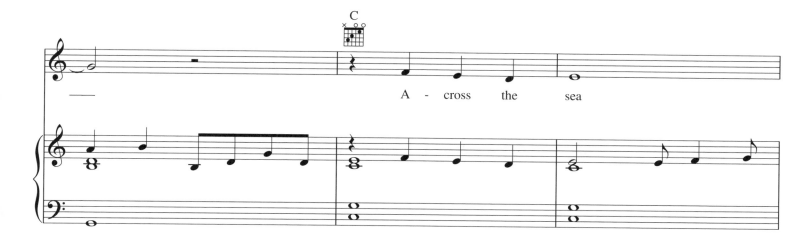

_____ A - cross the sea

a pale moon ris - es. The ships have

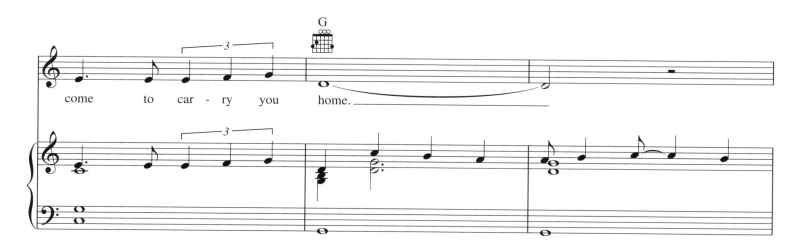

come to car - ry you home. _____

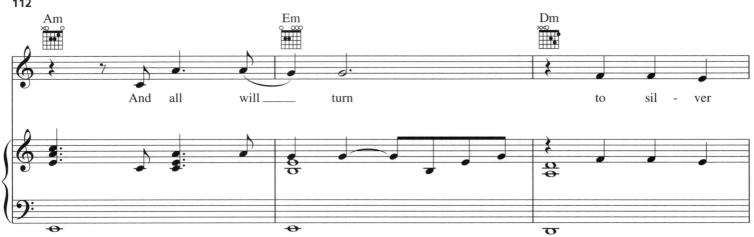

And all will ___ turn to sil - ver

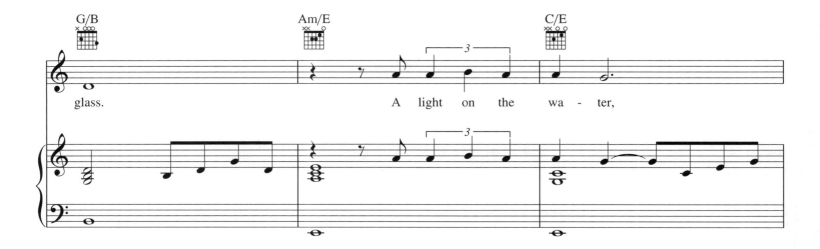

glass. A light on the wa - ter,

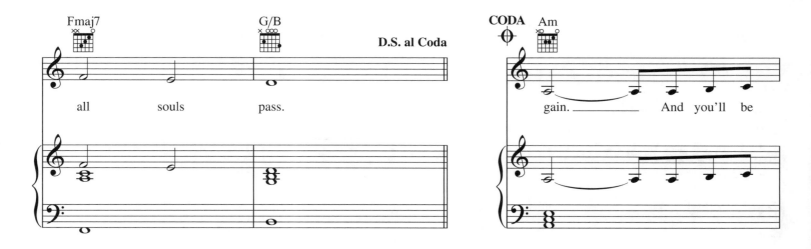

all souls pass.

D.S. al Coda

CODA

gain. ___ And you'll be

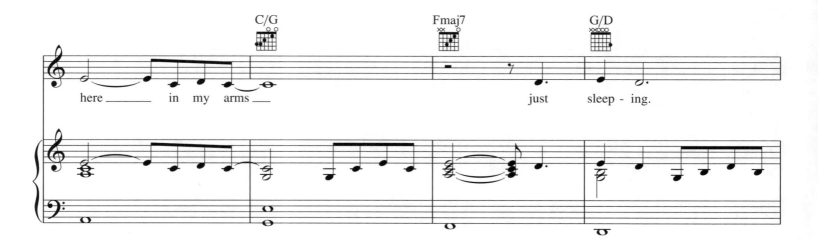

here ___ in my arms ___ just sleep - ing.

What can you see on the ho - ri - zon?

Why do the white gulls call? _____

A - cross the sea a pale moon

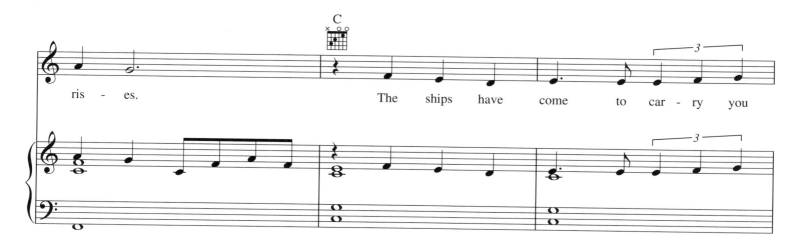

ris - es. The ships have come to car - ry you

home. _____ And all will __ turn

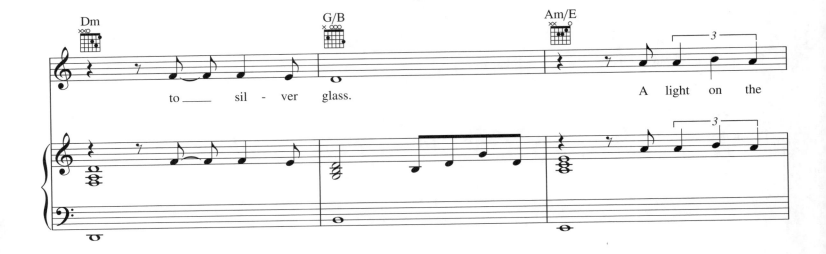

to ____ sil - ver glass. A light on the

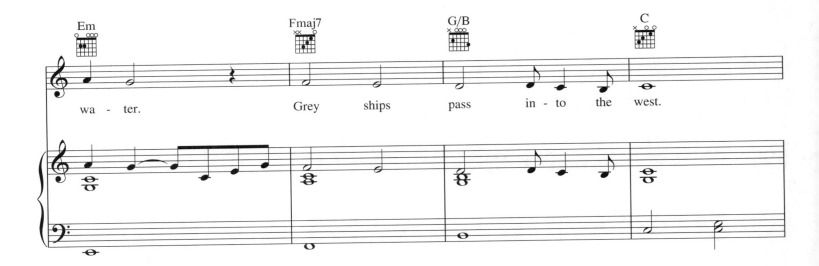

wa - ter. Grey ships pass in - to the west.

IT'S SO HARD TO SAY GOODBYE TO YESTERDAY

Words and Music by FREDDIE PERREN
and CHRISTINE YARIAN

How do I _____ say good-bye _____ to what _ we had? _____
know _____ where this road _____ is going to lead. _____

The good times _____ that made us laugh _____ out-weighed the
All I know _____ is where we've been _____ and what we've

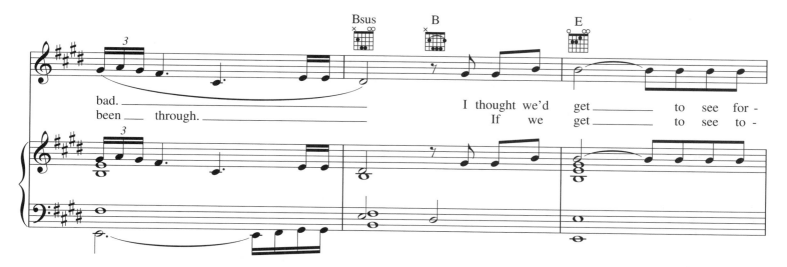

bad. _____
been _____ through. _____

I thought we'd get _____ to see for-
If we get _____ to see to-

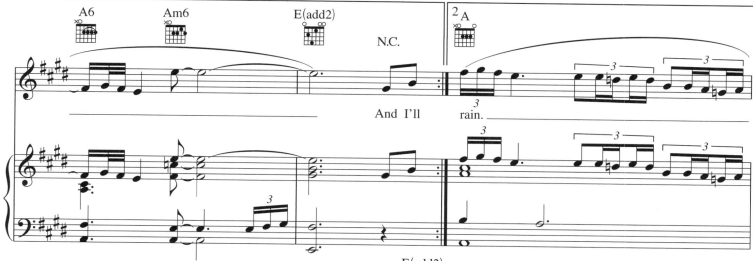

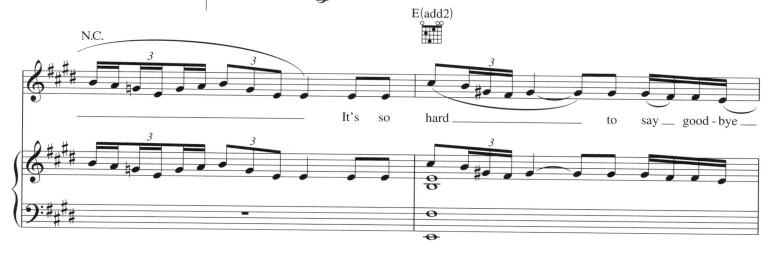

LET IT BE

Words and Music by JOHN LENNON
and PAUL McCARTNEY

Slowly

When I find my-self __ in times of trou-ble

Instrumental

Moth-er Mar-y comes to me speak-ing words of wis-dom; let it be. __ And in my hour of dark-ness, she is

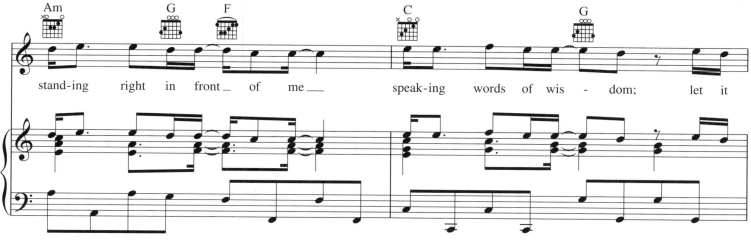

stand-ing right in front _ of me _ speak-ing words of wis - dom; let it

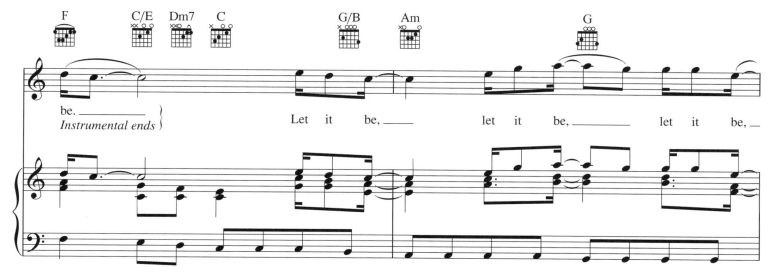

be. _____
Instrumental ends }   Let it be, _____ let it be, _____ let it be, _

_____ let it be. _____ Whis-per words _ of wis - dom; let it be. _

{ And when _____ the bro - ken - heart - ed peo - ple
{ And when _____ the night _ is cloud - y, there is

120

let it be. _____ There will be ___ an an - swer; let it be. _

Let it be, ___ let it be, _____ let it be, __

let it be. __

Whis - per words ___ of wis - dom; let it be. __
There will be ____ an an - swer; let it be. _

To Coda

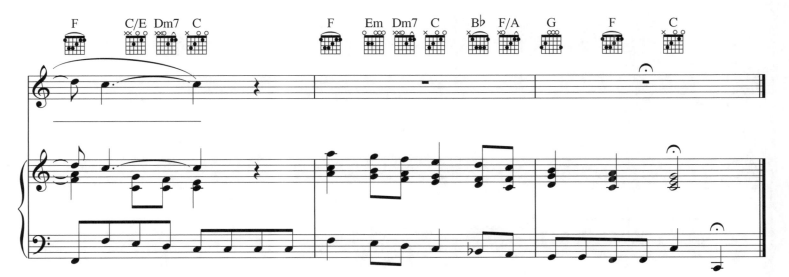

LIKE A RIVER

Words and Music by
CARLY SIMON

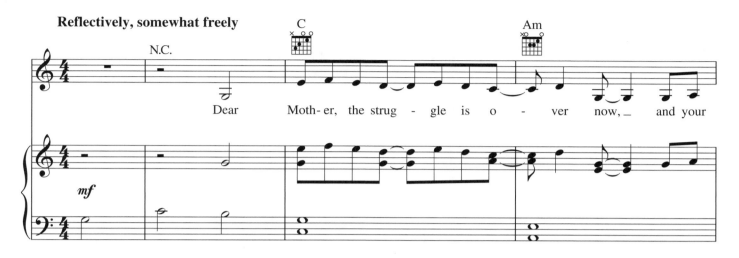

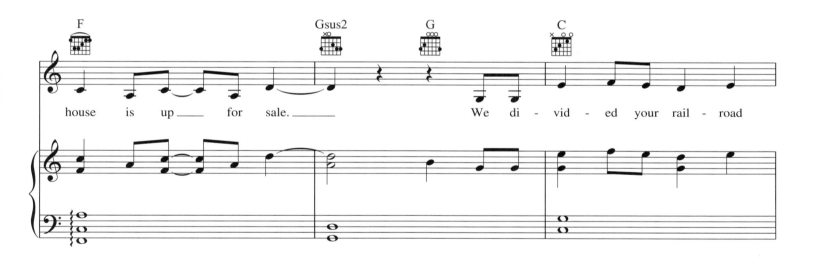

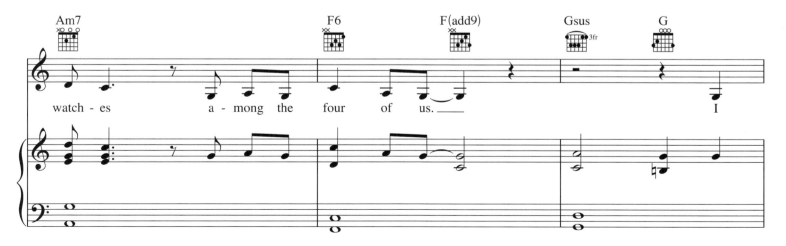

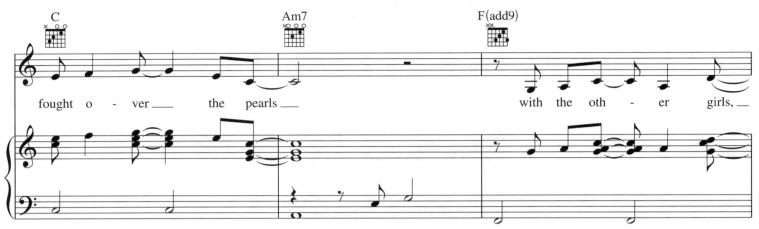

fought o - ver ___ the pearls ___ with the oth - er girls, ___

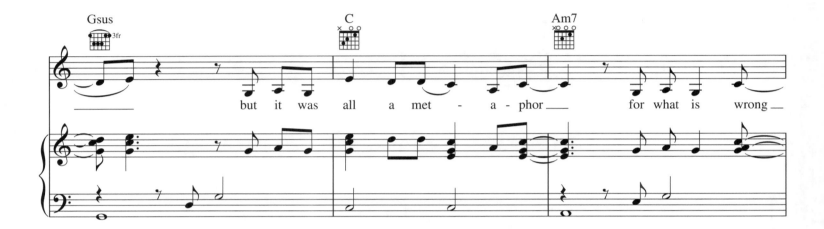

___ but it was all a met - a - phor ___ for what is wrong ___

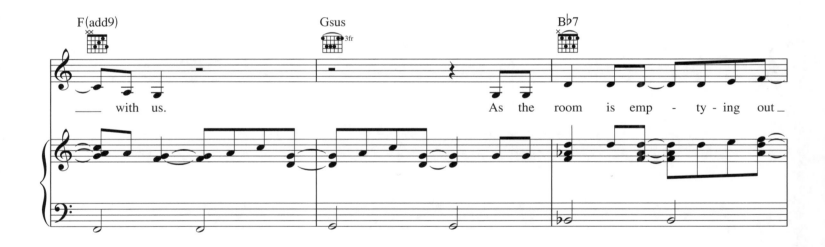

___ with us. As the room is emp - ty - ing out ___

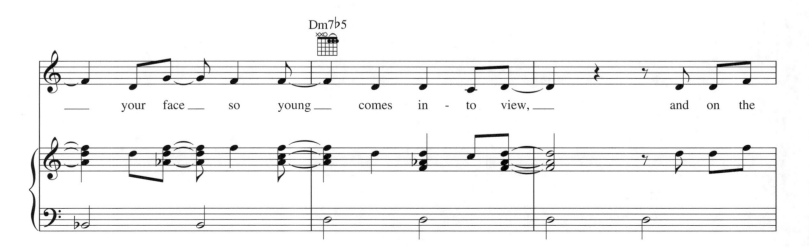

___ your face so young ___ comes in - to view, ___ and on the

back porch is a well - worn step __ and a pool of light __ that you can

walk in - to. __ I'll wait no more for __ you

like a daugh - ter.

like a daugh - ter. That part of our life __

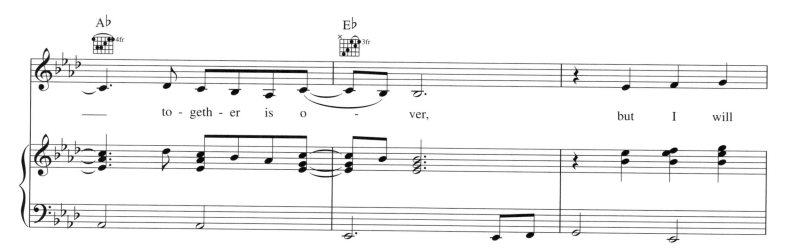

__ to - geth - er is o - ver, but I will

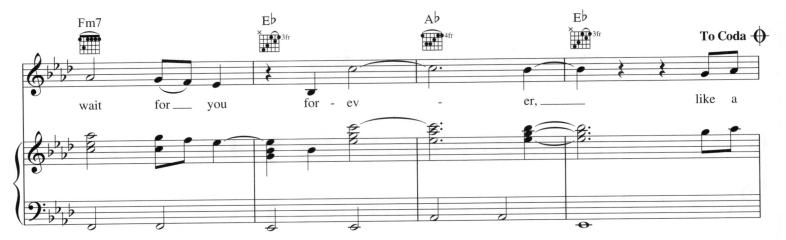

wait for ___ you for - ev - er, ___ like a

To Coda

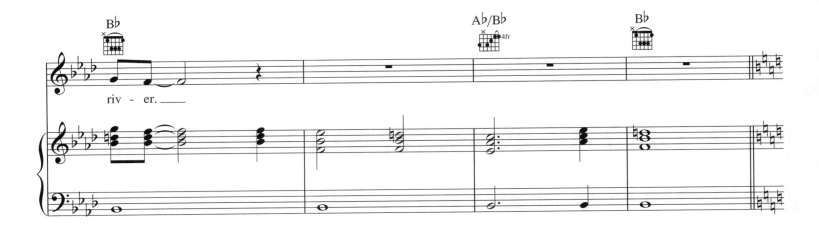

riv - er. ___

Steady tempo

Can you

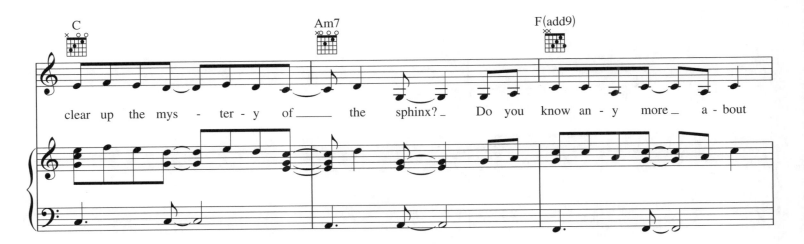

clear up the mys - ter - y of ___ the sphinx? __ Do you know an - y more __ a - bout

And I thought you touched my feet, ___ I ___ so want-

-ed it to be true. ___ And in my ___ thea-ter ___ there is ___

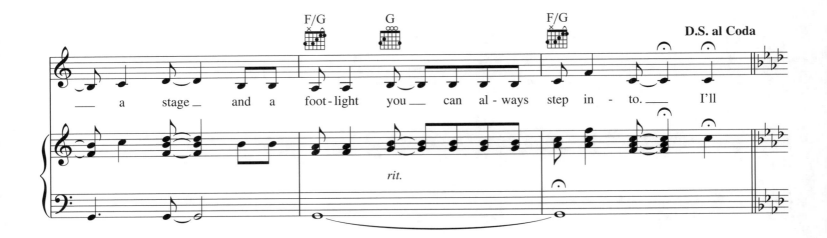

___ a stage ___ and a foot-light you ___ can al-ways step in-to. ___ I'll

D.S. al Coda

rit.

CODA

riv - er. ___

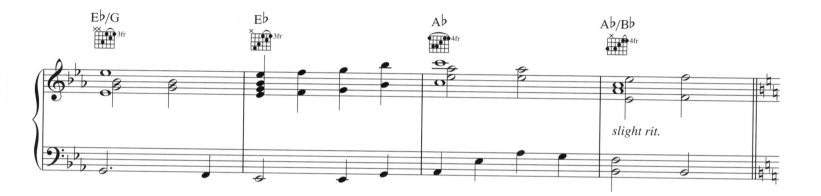

In the riv-er I know__ I will find____ the key__ and your voice__

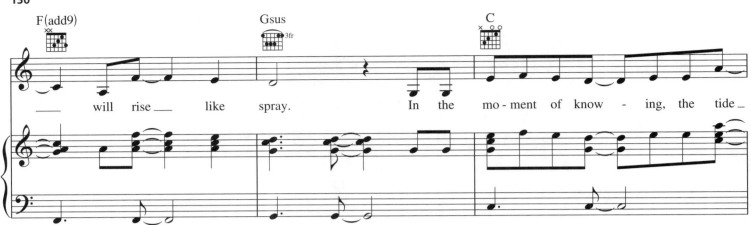

will rise ___ like spray. In the mo-ment of know-ing, the tide ___

will wash a-way my doubt. ___ 'Cause

Slower

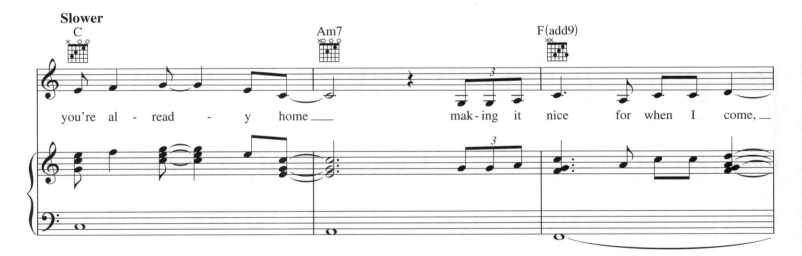

you're al-read-y home ___ mak-ing it nice for when I come, ___

Steady tempo

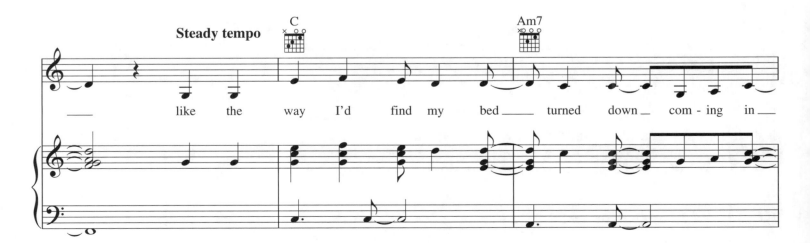

___ like the way I'd find my bed ___ turned down ___ com-ing in ___

from a late night out. Please keep re- mind- ing me—

— of what in— my soul— I know— is true.— Come in my boat,—

— there— is a seat— be- side me and two or three stars— that we can

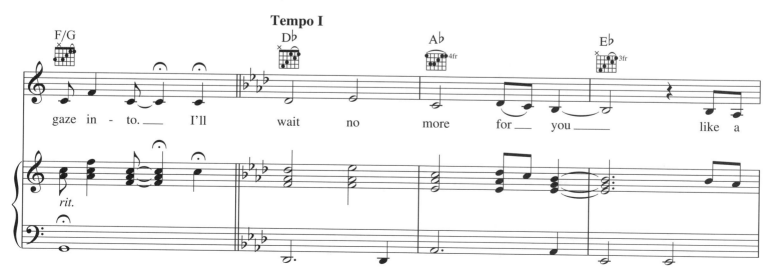

Tempo I

gaze in- to.— I'll wait no more for— you—— like a

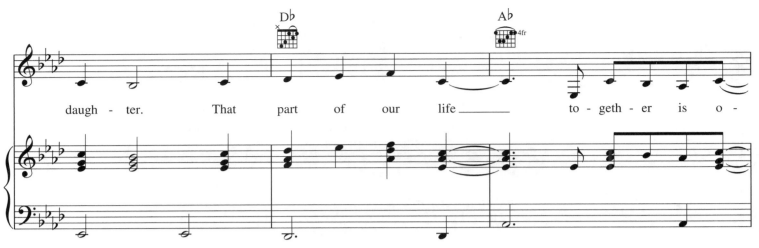

daugh - ter. That part of our life _____ to - geth - er is o -

- ver, but I will wait for ____ you ____

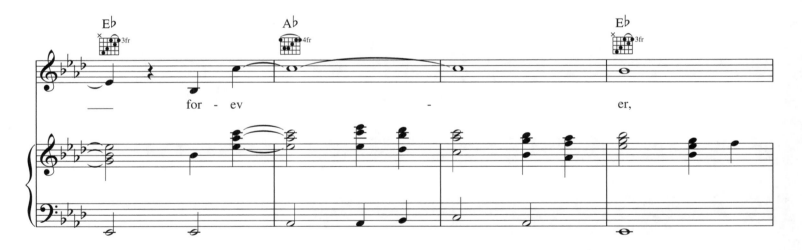

____ for - ev - er,

Slower

like a riv - er. ____

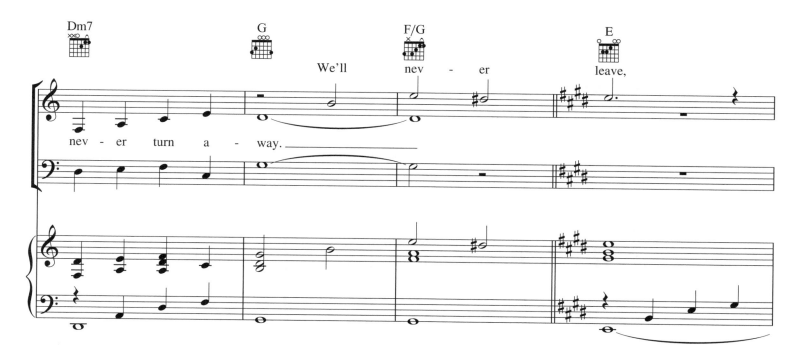

al - ways just a thought a - way, a can - dle al - ways

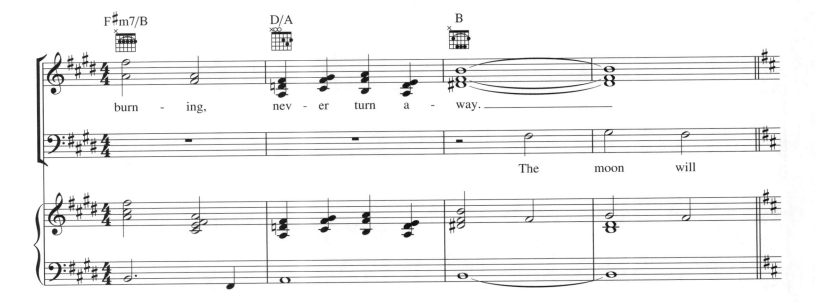

burn - ing, nev - er turn a - way.

The moon will

We'll nev - er leave, al - ways just a thought a - way,

hide, the dance will end, but in the

a can - dle al - ways burn - ing.

wind the tree _____ will bend. _____

I'm right be - side you.

I'm right be - side you.

I'll nev - er

I'm right be - side you.

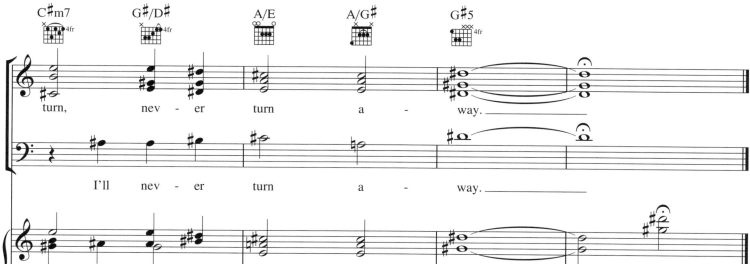

turn, nev - er turn a - way. _____

I'll nev - er turn a - way. _____

MY HEART WILL GO ON
(Love Theme from 'Titanic')
from the Paramount and Twentieth Century Fox Motion Picture TITANIC

Music by JAMES HORNER
Lyric by WILL JENNINGS

Moderately

Ev - 'ry night in my dreams I see you, I

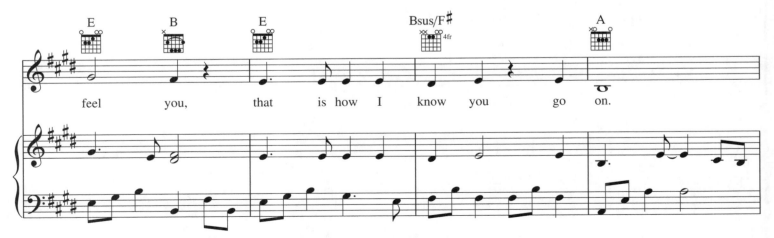

feel you, that is how I know you go on.

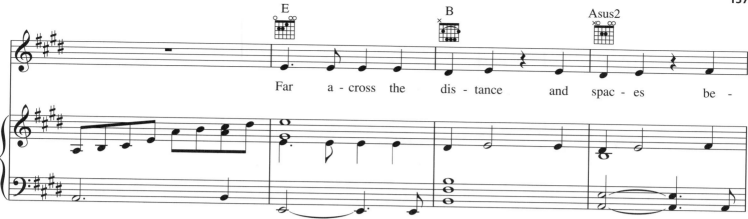

Far a-cross the dis-tance and spac-es be-

tween us, you have come to show you go on.

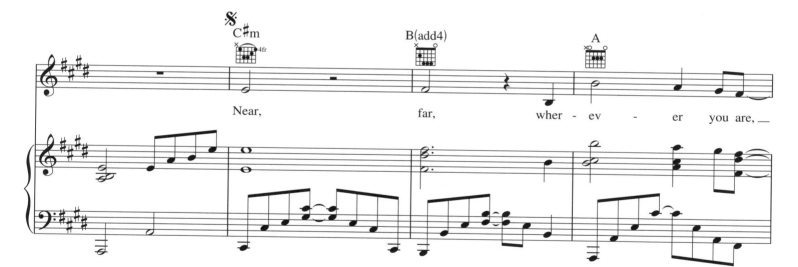

Near, far, wher-ev-er you are, __

__ I be-lieve that the heart does go on. __

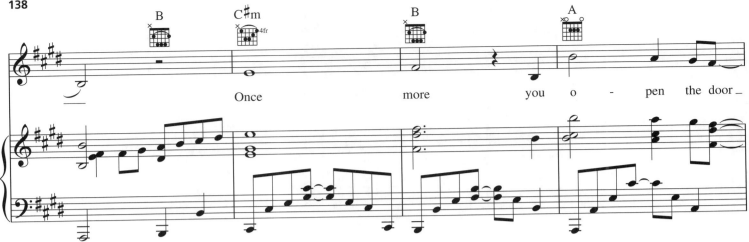

Once more you o - pen the door

and you're here in my heart, and my heart will go

To Coda

on and on.

Love can touch us one time and last for a

life - time, and nev - er let go till we're gone.

Love was when I loved you; one true time I

hold to. In my life we'll al - ways go on.

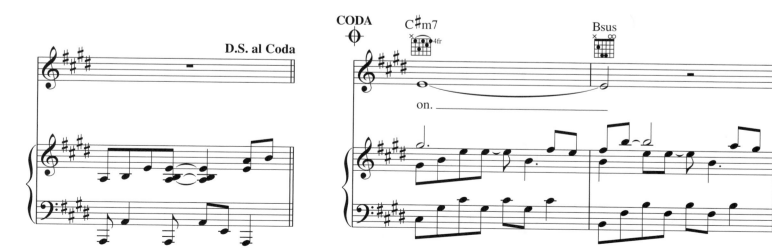

D.S. al Coda

CODA

on. _____

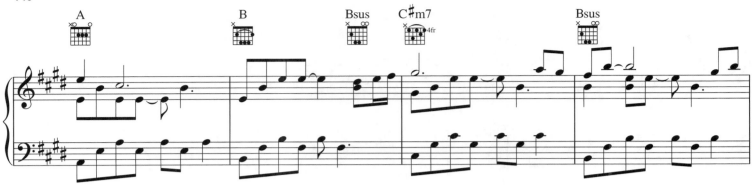

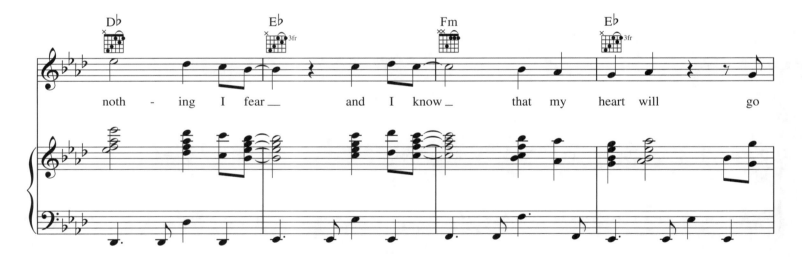

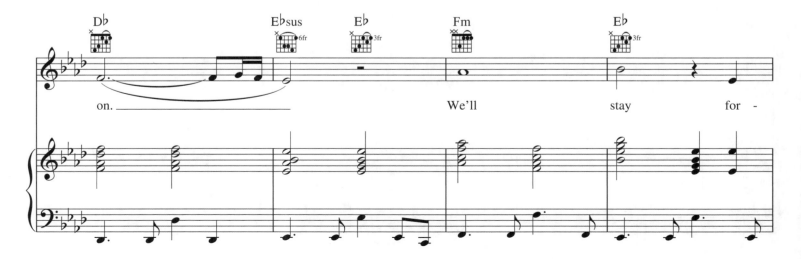

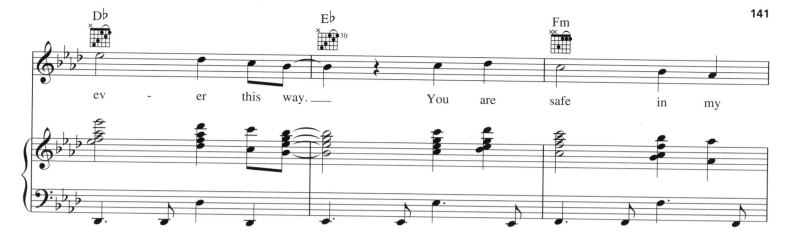

ev - er this way. ___ You are safe in my

heart, and my heart will go on and on. ___

ff *decrescendo to end*

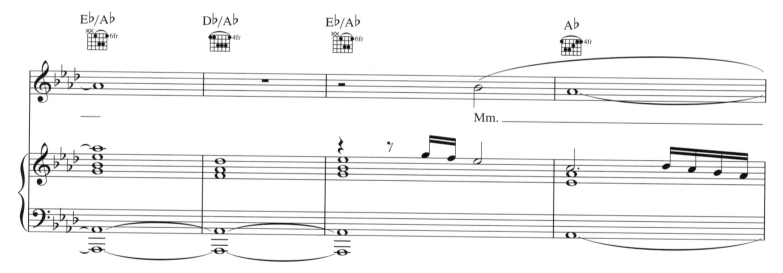

Mm. ___

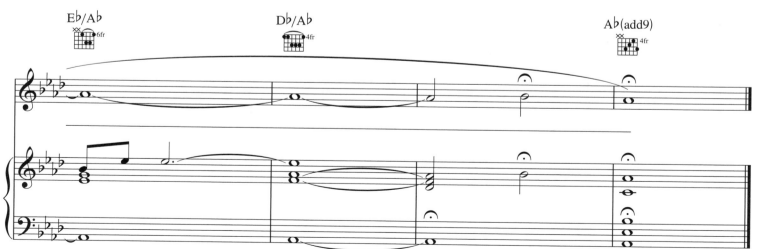

ONE MORE DAY
(With You)

Words and Music by STEVEN DALE JONES
and BOBBY TOMERLIN

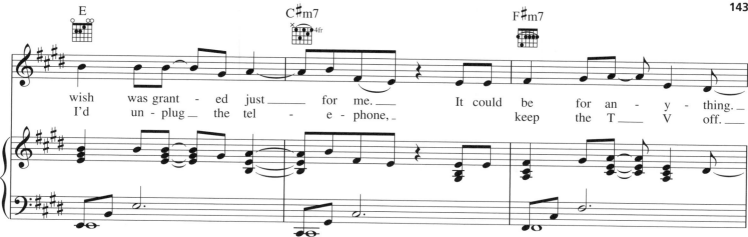

wish was grant - ed just _____ for me. _____ It could be for an - y - thing. _____
I'd un - plug _____ the tel - e - phone, _____ keep the T _____ V off. _____

_____ I did - n't ask for mon - ey or a
_____ I'd hold _____ you ev - 'ry sec - ond, say a

man - sion on Mal - i - bu. _____ I sim - ply wished _____ for
mil - lion "I _____ love you's." _____ It's what I'd do _____ with

one more day _____ with you. _____
one more day _____ with you. _____

One _____ more day, _____

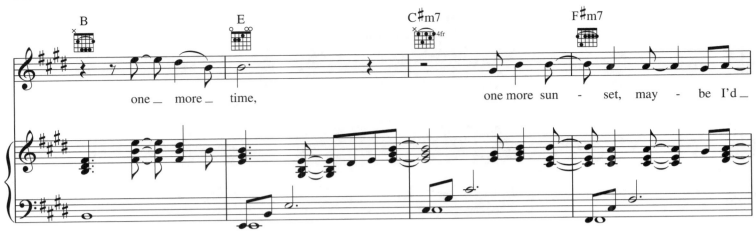

one __ more __ time, one more sun - set, may - be I'd __

__ be sat - is - fied. __ But then __ a - gain, ___ I know __

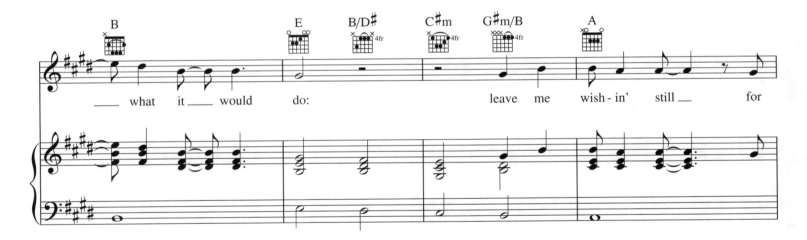

__ what it __ would do: leave me wish - in' still __ for

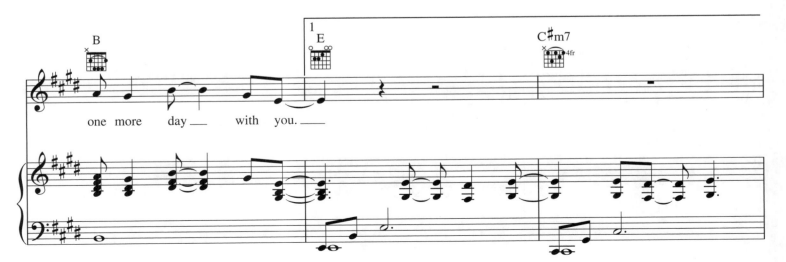

one more day __ with you. __

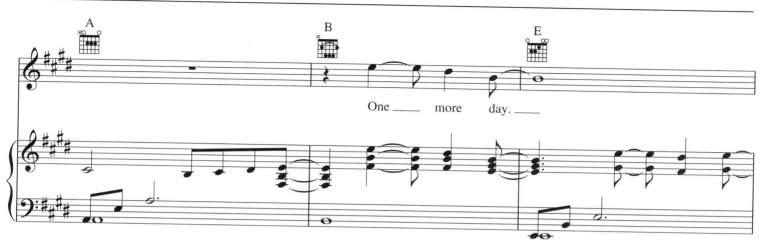

One _____ more day. _____

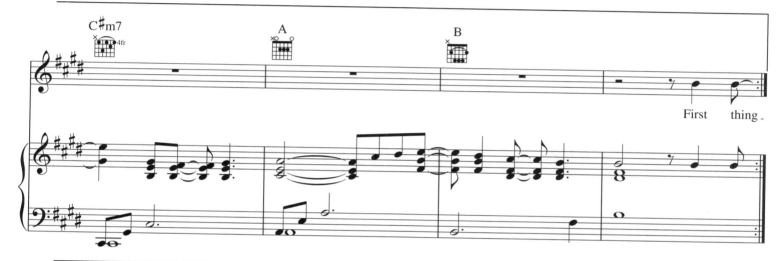

First thing _

One _____ more day, _____

one _____ more _____ time,   one more sun -

- set, may - be I'd ___ be sat - is - fied. ___

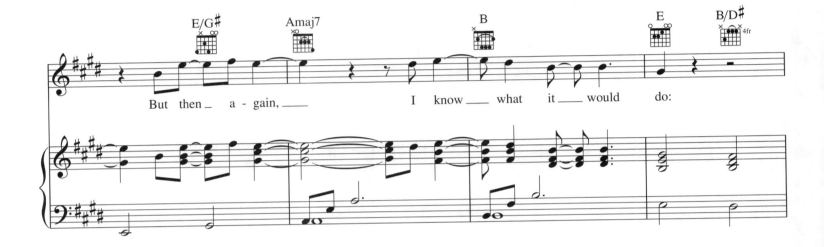

But then _ a - gain, ___ I know ___ what it ___ would do:

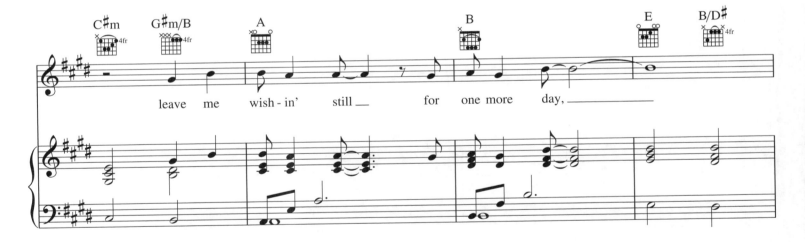

leave me wish - in' still ___ for one more day, ___

leave me wish - in' still ___ for one more day, ___

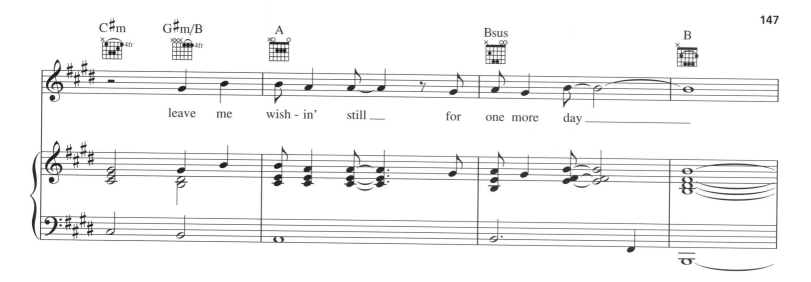

leave me wish-in' still ___ for one more day ___

with you. ___

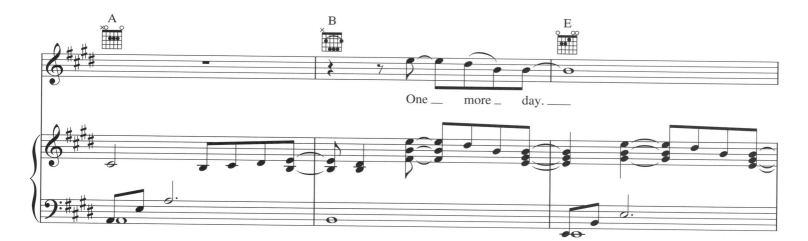

One ___ more ___ day. ___

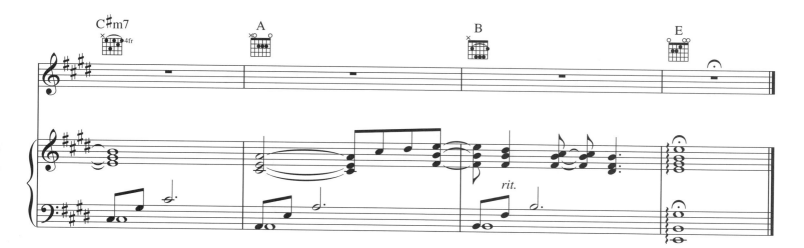

rit.

ONE SWEET DAY

Words and Music by MARIAH CAREY,
WALTER AFANASIEFF, MICHAEL McCARY,
NATHAN MORRIS, SHAWN STOCKMAN
and WANYA MORRIS

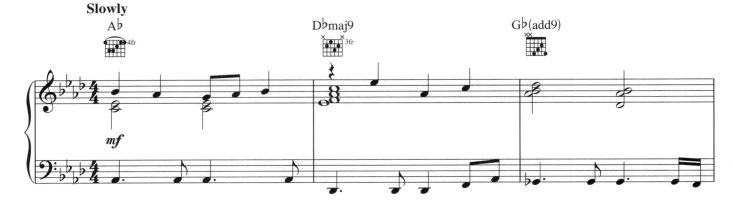

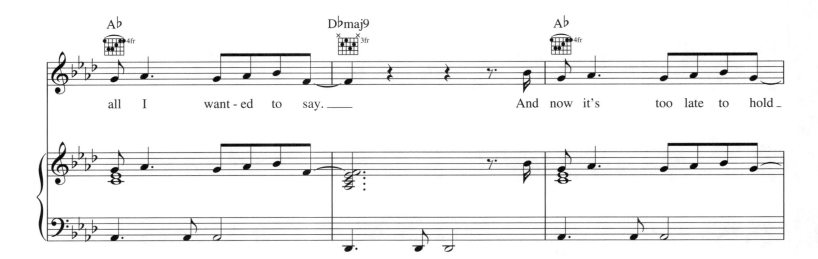

know you're shin-ing down on me from heav-en, _____ like so

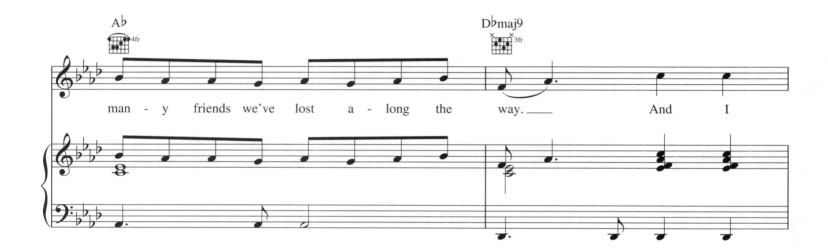

man-y friends we've lost a-long the way. _____ And I

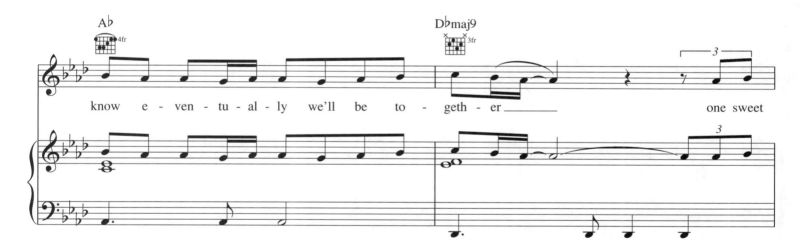

know e-ven-tu-al-ly we'll be to-geth-er _____ one sweet

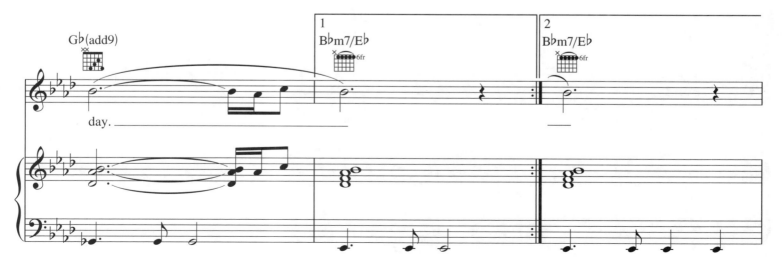

day. _____

Although the sun will nev-er shine the same,

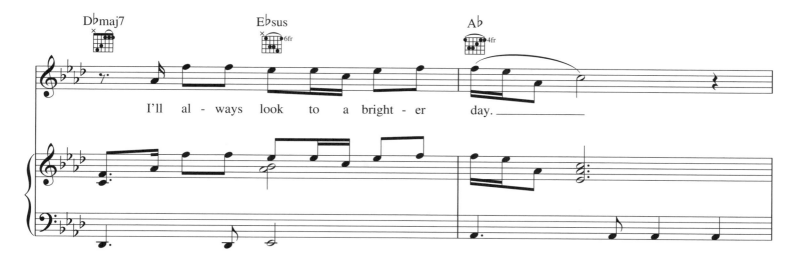

I'll al-ways look to a bright-er day.

Lord, I know when I lay me down to sleep,

You will al-ways lis-ten as I pray. And I

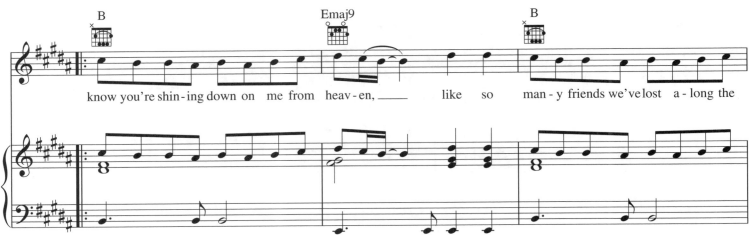

know you're shin-ing down on me from heav-en, _____ like so man-y friends we've lost a - long the

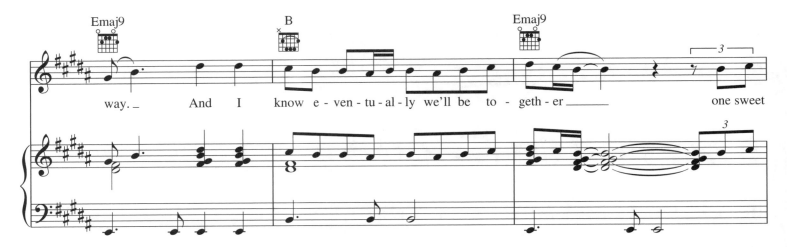

way. _ And I know e - ven - tu - al - ly we'll be to - geth - er _____ one sweet

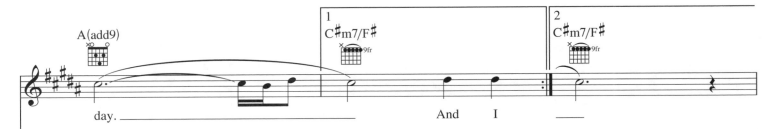

day. _____ And I _____

Sor - ry I nev - er told _____ you _ all I want-ed to say. _____

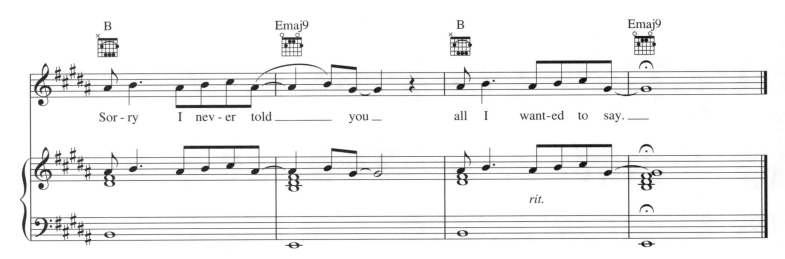

TEARS IN HEAVEN

Words and Music by ERIC CLAPTON
and WILL JENNINGS

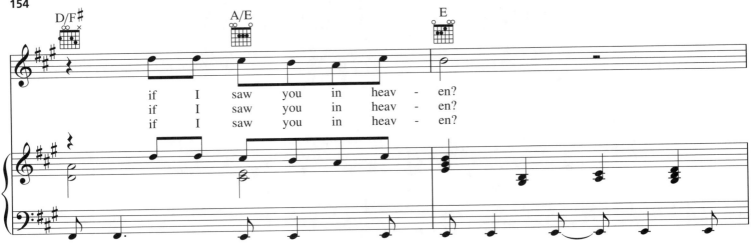

if I saw you in heav - en?
if I saw you in heav - en?
if I saw you in heav - en?

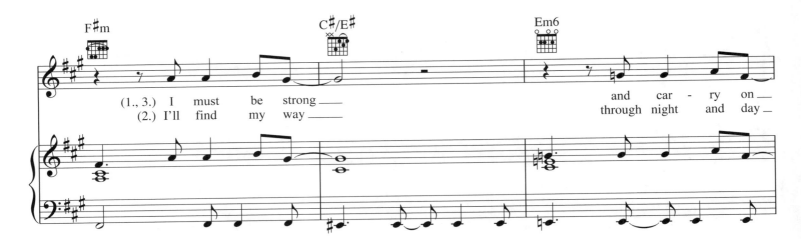

(1., 3.) I must be strong ___ and car - ry on ___
(2.) I'll find my way ___ through night and day ___

'cause I know ___ I don't be - long ___
'cause I know ___ I just can't stay ___

here in heav - en.
here in heav - en.

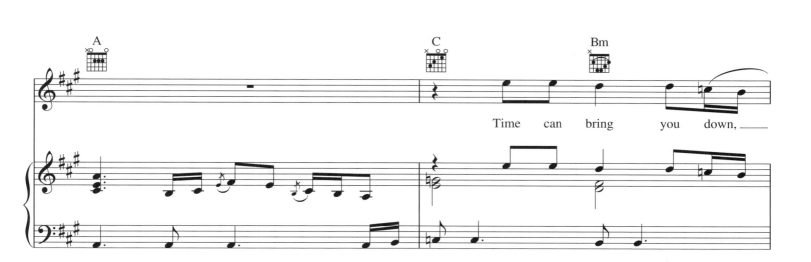

Time can bring you down, _____

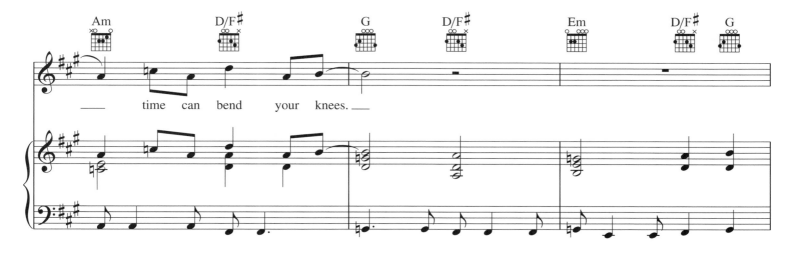

_____ time can bend your knees. _____

Time can break the heart, _____ have you beg - gin' please, _____ beg - gin' please. _

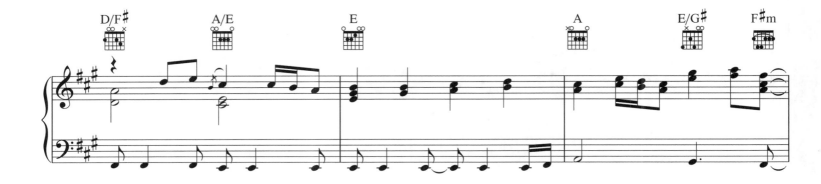

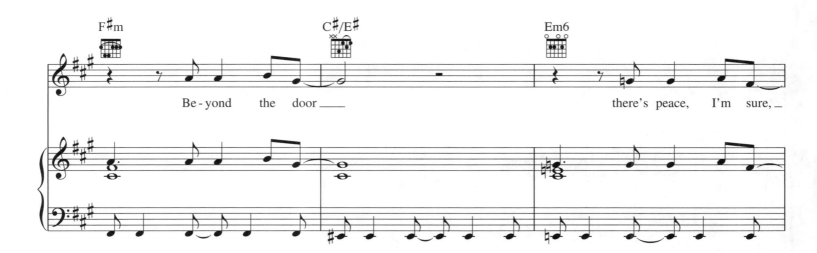

Be - yond the door _____ there's peace, I'm sure, _

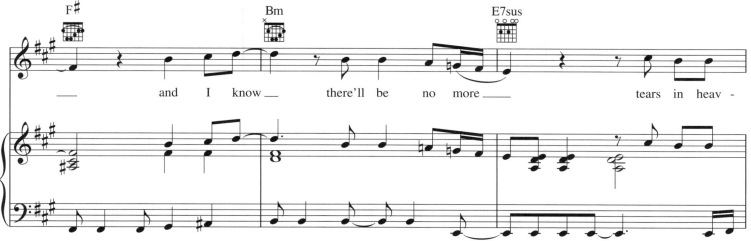

and I know ___ there'll be no more ___ tears in heav-

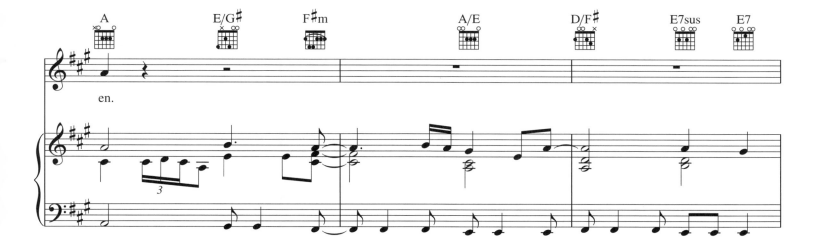

en.

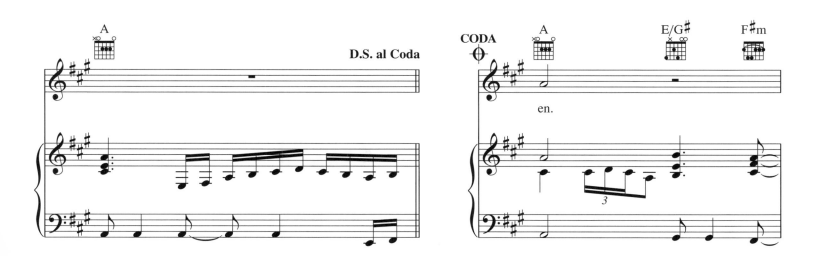

D.S. al Coda

CODA

en.

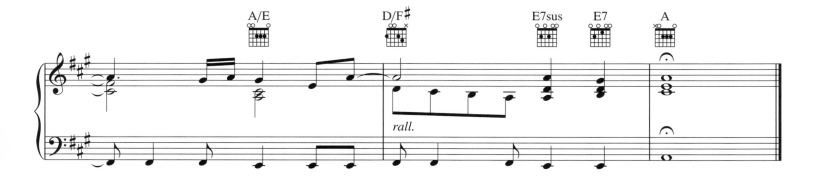

rall.

REMEMBER ME THIS WAY

from the Universal Motion Picture CASPER

Music by DAVID FOSTER
Lyrics by LINDA THOMPSON

Moderately slow

Ev - 'ry now _ and then _ we find _ a spe - cial

friend who nev - er lets _ us down, _ who un - der - stands _ it all, reach - es out each time you fall. _

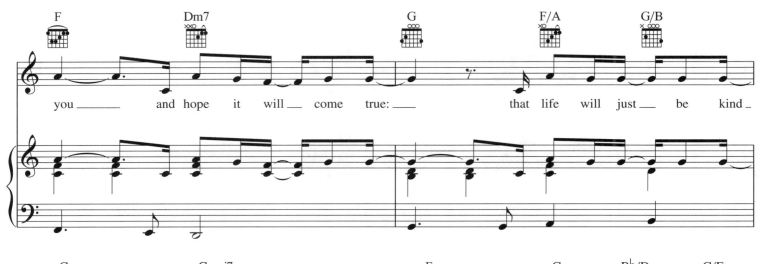

you _____ and hope it will __ come true: ___ that life will just __ be kind _

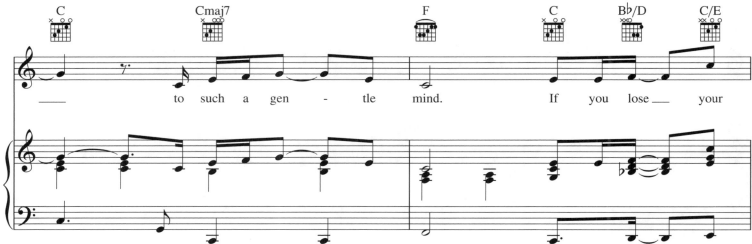

_____ to such a gen - tle mind. If you lose __ your

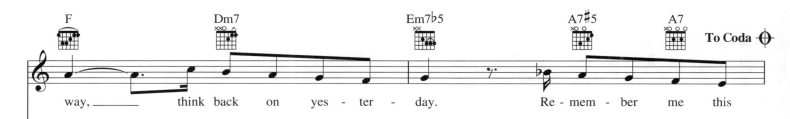

way, _____ think back on yes - ter - day. Re - mem - ber me this

To Coda ⊕

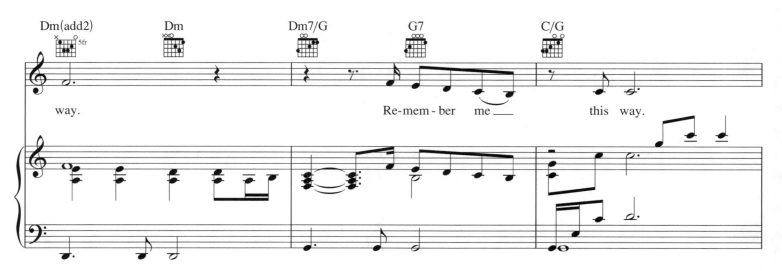

way. Re - mem - ber me __ this way.

I don't need eyes __ to see the love __ you bring to

D.S. al Coda

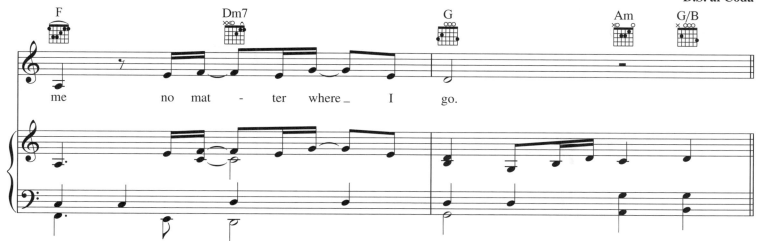

me no mat - ter where __ I go.

CODA

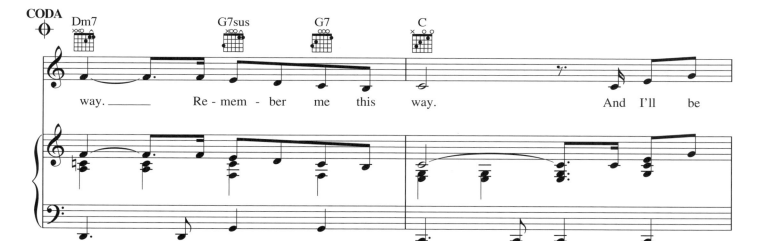

way. _____ Re - mem - ber me this way. And I'll be

right be - hind __ your shoul - der watch - ing you. I'll be

stand - ing by ___ your side ___ in all ___ you ___ do. And I won't ev - er

leave, as long as you be - lieve. You just _____ be - lieve. ___

___ I'll make a wish ___ for you _____ and hope it will ___ come true: ___

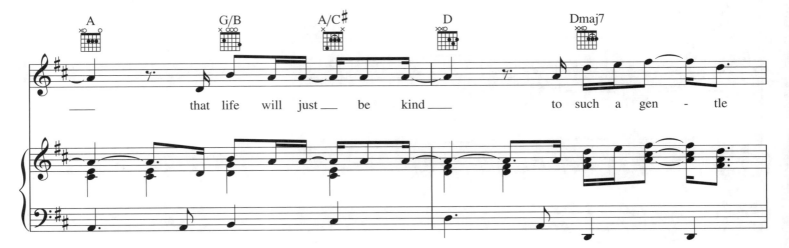

___ that life will just ___ be kind _____ to such a gen - tle

SINCE I LOST YOU

Words and Music by TONY BANKS,
PHIL COLLINS and MIKE RUTHERFORD

Moderately slow

It seems in a mo - ment, your whole world can shat -
It's all too eas - y to take so much for grant -

Instrumental

ter.
ed,

Like morn - ing dreams,
but it's so hard to

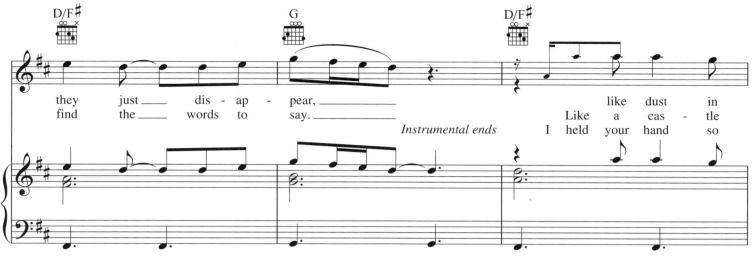

they   just ____ dis - ap - pear, _____ like   dust   in

find   the ____ words   to   say. _____

Instrumental ends   I   held   your   hand   so

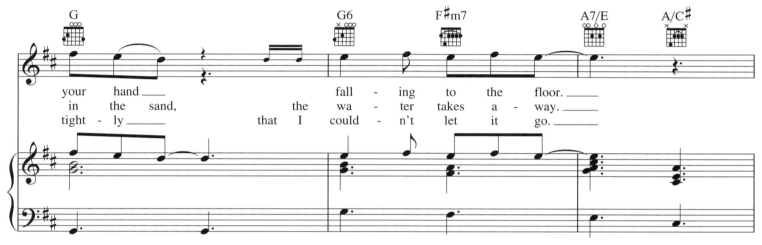

your   hand _____ fall - ing   to   the   floor. ____

in   the   sand, _____ the   wa - ter   takes   a - way. ____

tight - ly _____ that   I   could - n't   let   it   go.

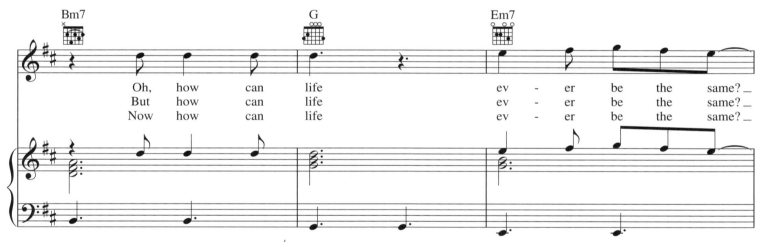

Oh,   how   can   life _____ ev - er   be   the   same? _

But   how   can   life _____ ev - er   be   the   same? _

Now   how   can   life _____ ev - er   be   the   same? _

To Coda

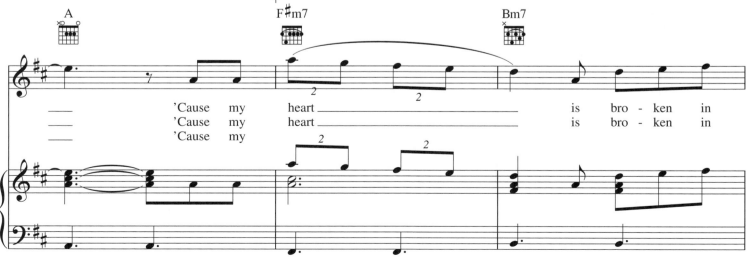

____ 'Cause   my   heart _____ is   bro - ken   in

____ 'Cause   my   heart _____ is   bro - ken   in

____ 'Cause   my

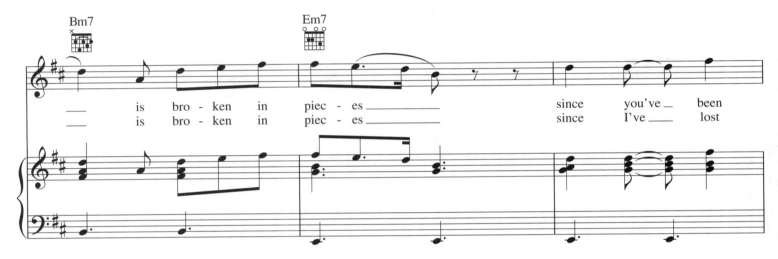

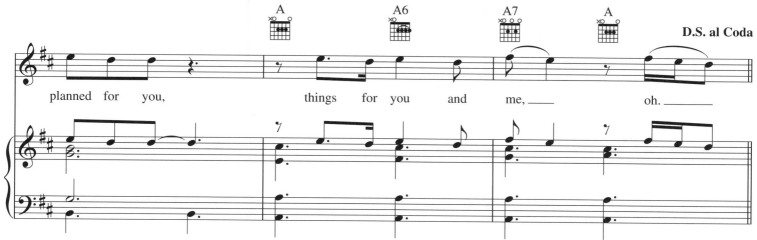

D.S. al Coda

planned for you, things for you and me, _____ oh. _____

CODA

heart _____ is bro - ken in piec - es. _____ Yes, my

heart _____ is bro - ken in piec - es _____ since you've _ been

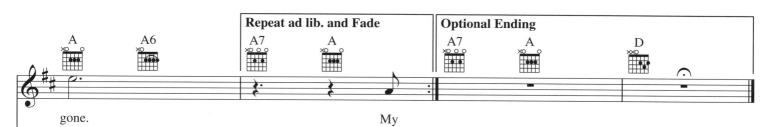

Repeat ad lib. and Fade

Optional Ending

gone. My

SLIPPED AWAY

Words and Music by AVRIL LAVIGNE
and CHANTAL KREVIAZUK

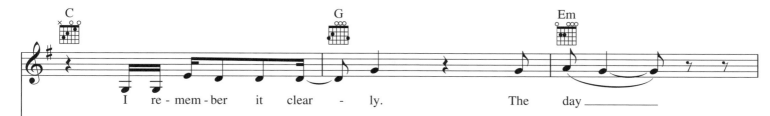

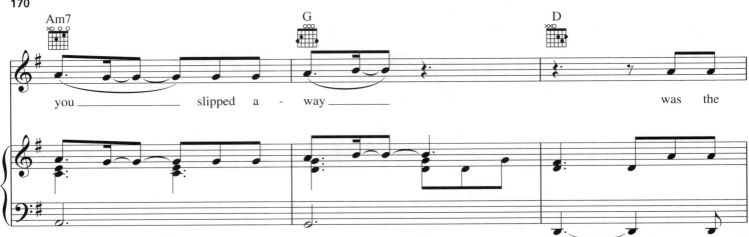

you _____ slipped a - way _____ was the

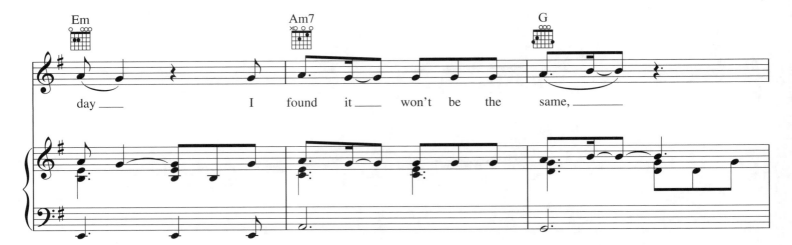

day ___ I found it ___ won't be the same, _____

oh. _____ Na na. ___

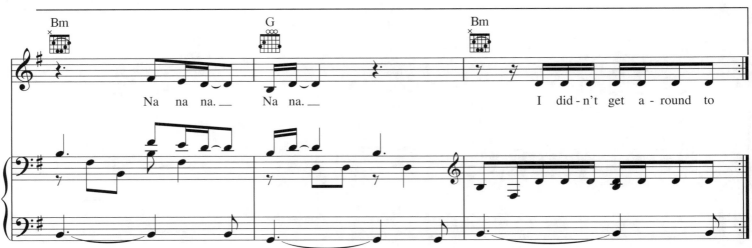

Na na na. ___ Na na. ___ I did-n't get a - round to

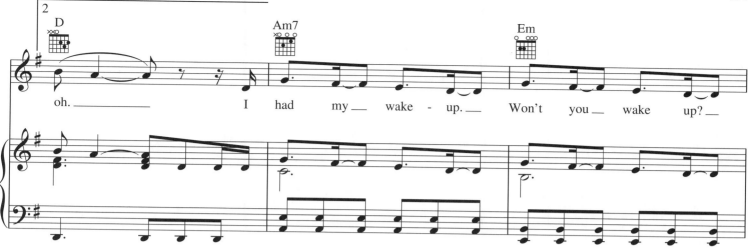

oh. _____ I had my __ wake - up. __ Won't you __ wake up? __

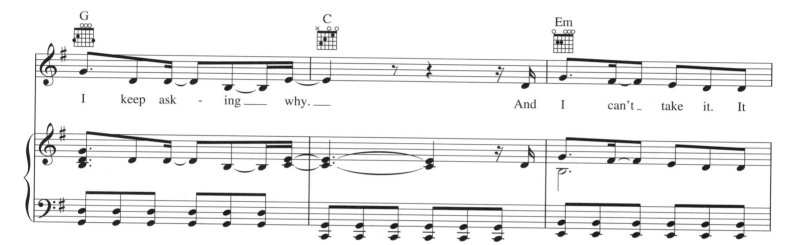

I keep ask - ing __ why. __ And I can't __ take it. It

was - n't __ fake. It, it hap - pened. __ You passed by. ___

Now you're gone, now you're gone. There you go, there you go, some-where I can't bring you

back.   Now you're gone, now you're gone. There you go, there you go,

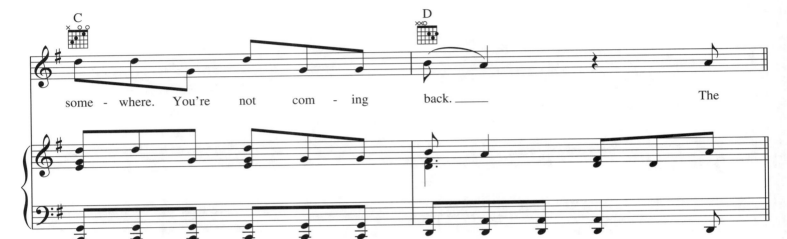

some - where. You're not com - ing   back. _____   The

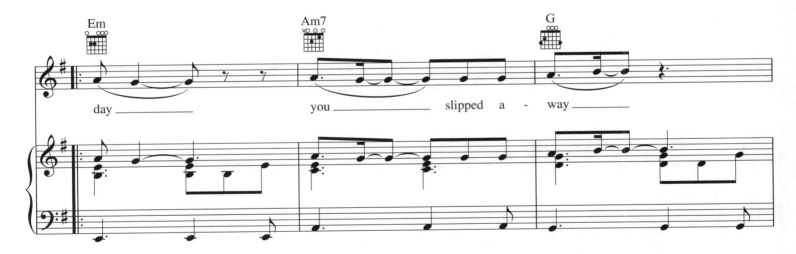

day _____   you _____ slipped a - way _____

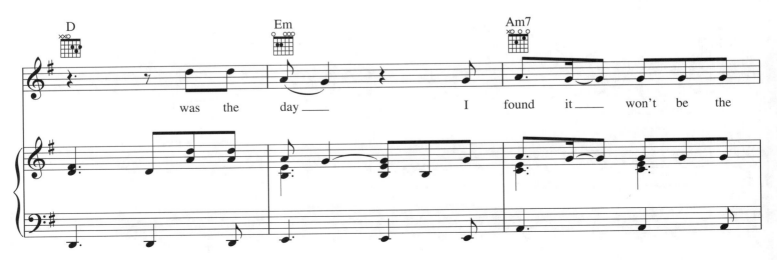

was the day ____   I found it ____ won't be the

SOMEONE'S WATCHING OVER ME

Words and Music by JOHN SHANKS
and KARA DioGUARDI

Recorded a half step lower.

THERE IS A REASON

Words and Music by
RON BLOCK

Easy Country Ballad

I've ___ seen hard ___ times, ___

and I've ___ been ___ told there is-n't an-y won-

-der that I fall. ___

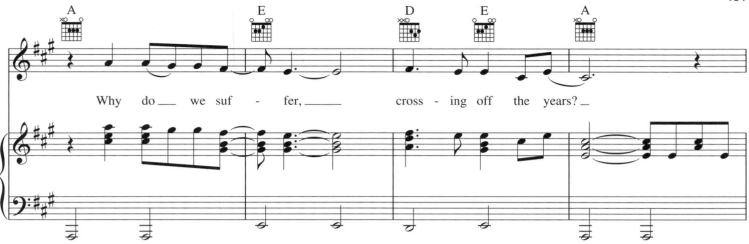

Why do we suf - fer, _____ cross - ing off the years? _____

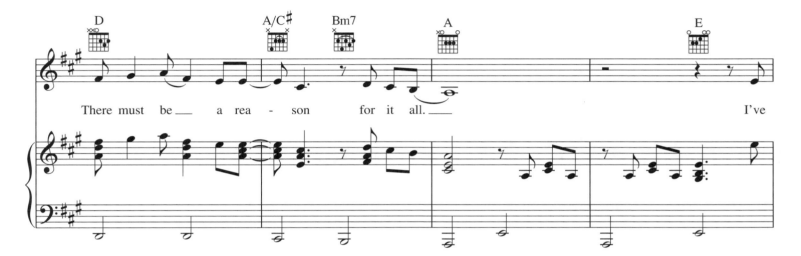

There must be _ a rea - son for it all. _____ I've

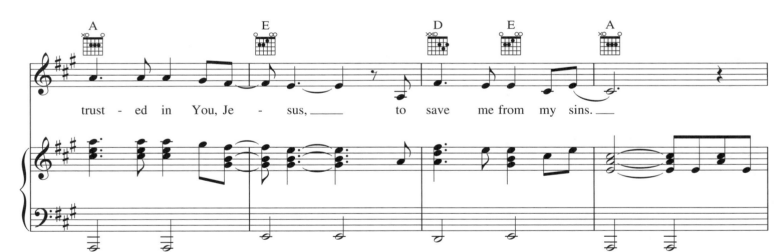

trust - ed in You, Je - sus, _____ to save me from my sins. _____

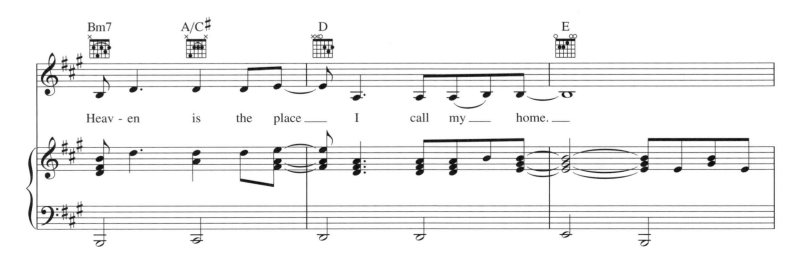

Heav - en is the place _____ I call my _____ home. _____

But I ___ keep on ___ get-ting caught ___ up in this

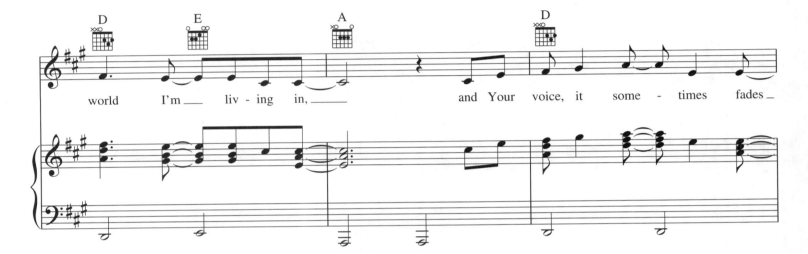

world I'm ___ liv-ing in, ___ and Your voice, it some-times fades ___

___ be-fore ___ I ___ know. ___

Hurt-ing brings ___ my heart ___ to You, ___ cry-ing with my ___ need, ___

de- pend - ing on ___ Your love ___ to car - ry me. ___

___ The love that shed His blood ___

___ for ___ all the world ___ to see, ___

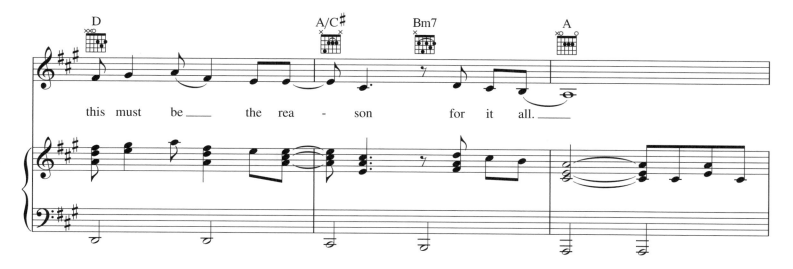

this must be ___ the rea - son for it all. ___

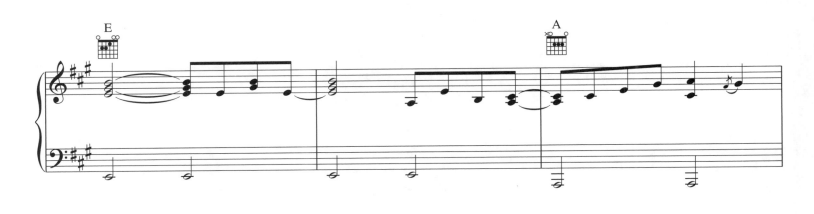

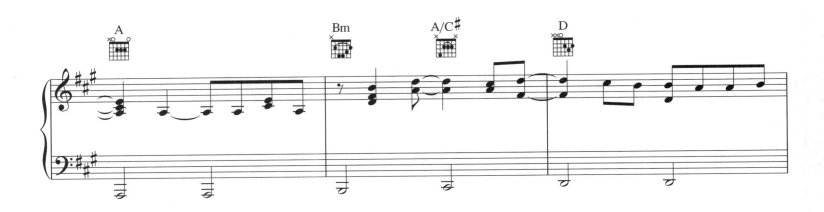

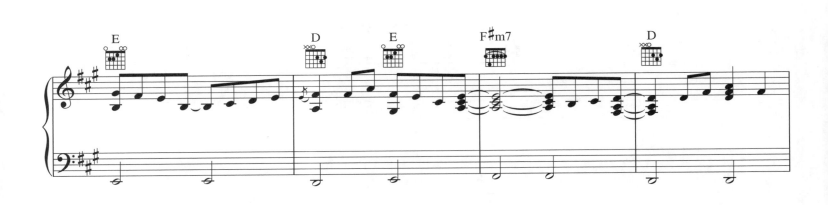

when the One who loves __ me most __ will give __ me all. __

D.S. al Coda   **CODA**

In

I've __ seen hard __ times, __ and I've __ been __

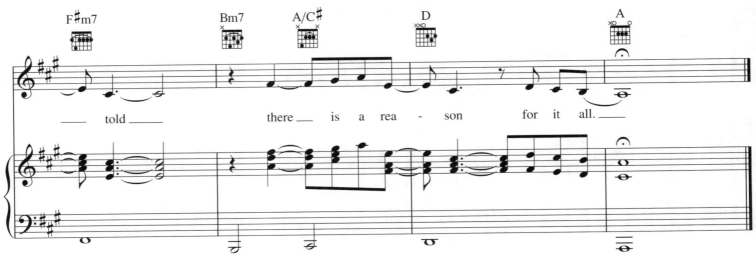

__ told __ there __ is a rea - son for it all. __

THERE YOU'LL BE

from Touchstone Pictures'/Jerry Bruckheimer Films' PEARL HARBOR

Words and Music by
DIANE WARREN

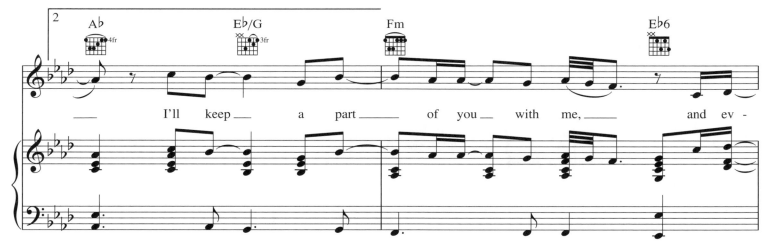

my strength, — and I wan-na thank you now — for all the ways

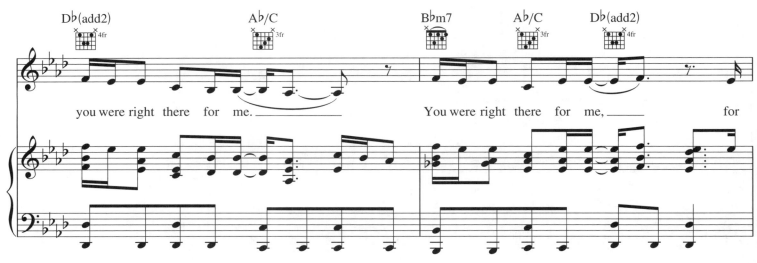

you were right there for me. _____ You were right there for me, _____ for

al - ways. _____ In my dreams I'll al - ways see you

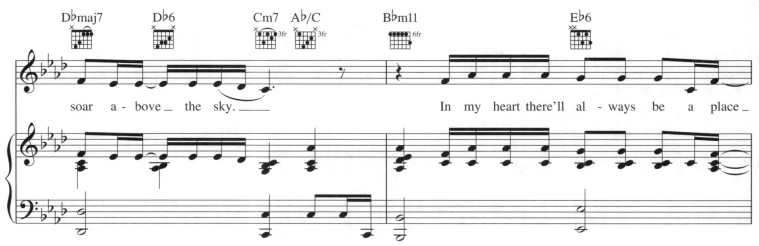

soar a - bove — the sky. _____ In my heart there'll al - ways be a place _____

for you for all my life. I'll keep a part

of you with me, and ev-'ry-where I am, there you'll be,

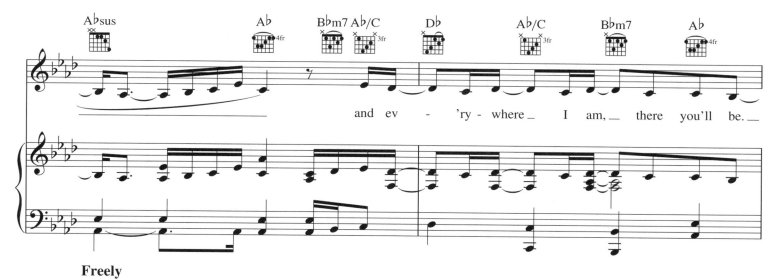

and ev-'ry-where I am, there you'll be.

Freely

There you'll be.

TIME TO SAY GOODBYE
(Con te partirò)

Words and Music by LUCIO QUARANTOTTO
and FRANCESCO SARTORI
English translation by FRANK PETERSON

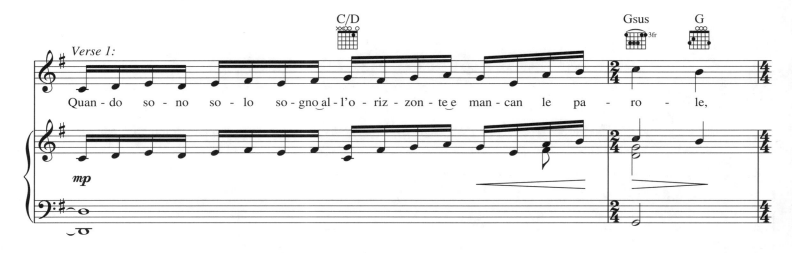

Verse 1:

Quan- do so- no so- lo so- gno al-l'o- riz- zon- te e man- can le pa- ro- le,

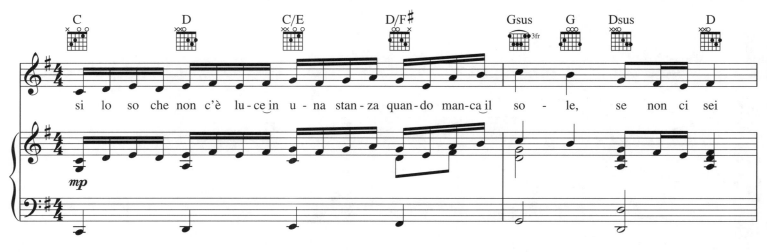

si lo so che non c'è lu- ce in u- na stan- za quan- do man- ca il so- le, se non ci sei

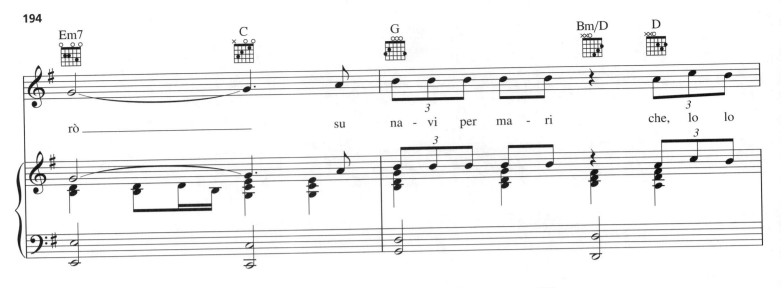

rò _____ su na - vi per ma - ri che, lo lo

so, no, no non e - si - sto - no più, con te io li vi - vrò. ____

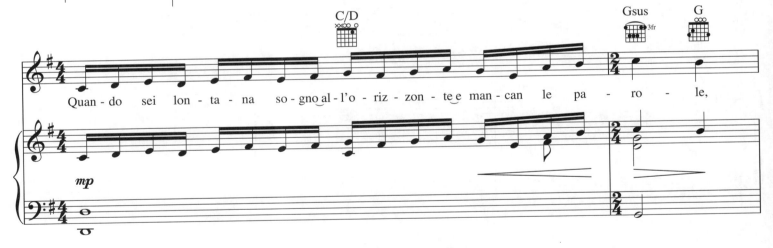

Quan - do sei lon - ta - na so - gno al - l'o - riz - zon - te e man - can le pa - ro - le,

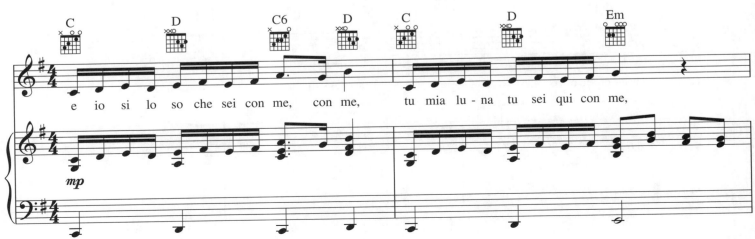

e io si lo so che sei con me, con me, tu mia lu - na tu sei qui con me,

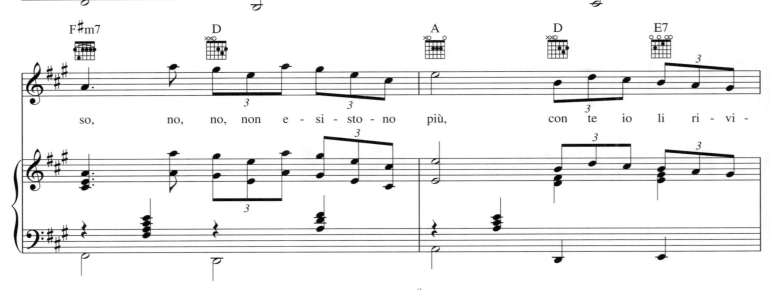

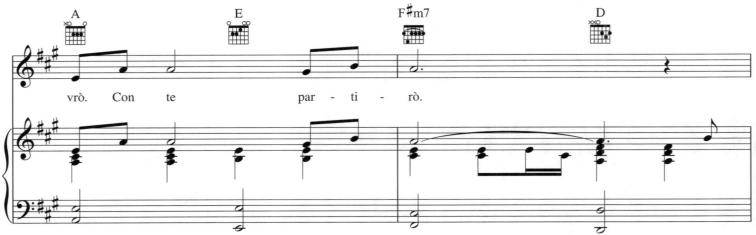

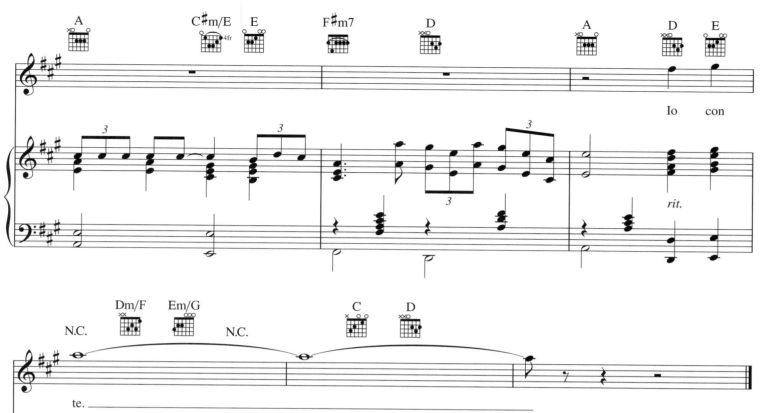

English literal translation:
Verse 1:
When I'm alone, I dream of the horizon and words fail me.
There is no light in a room where there is no sun.
And there is no sun if you're not here with me, with me.
From every window, unfurl my heart, the heart that you have won.
Into me you've poured the light, the light that you've found by the side of the road.

Chorus:
Time to say goodbye. Places that I've never seen or experienced with you,
Now I shall. I'll sail with you upon ships across the seas,
Seas that exist no more. It's time to say goodbye.

Verse 2:
When you're far away, I dream of the horizon and words fail me.
And of course, I know that you're with me, with me.
You, my moon, you are with me.
My sun, you're here with me, with me, with me, with me.

Chorus:
Time to say goodbye. Places that I've never seen or experienced with you,
Now I shall. I'll sail with you upon ships across the seas,
Seas that exist no more, I'll revive them with you.

Tag:
I'll go with you upon ships across the seas,
Seas that exist no more, I'll revive them with you.
I'll go with you, I'll go with you.

TOGETHER AGAIN

Words and Music by JANET JACKSON,
Terry Lewis and JAMES HARRIS III

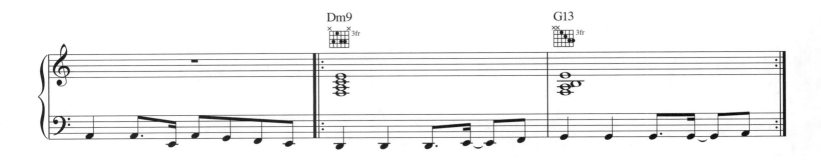

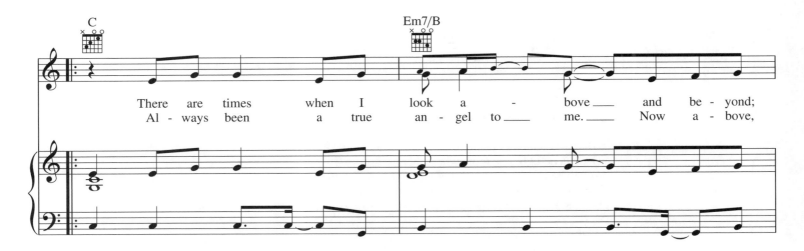

There are times when I look a - bove ___ and be - yond;
Al - ways been a true an - gel to ___ me. ___ Now a - bove,

there are times when I feel your love a - round ___ me, ba - by.
I can't wait for you to wrap your wings a - round ___ me, ba - by,

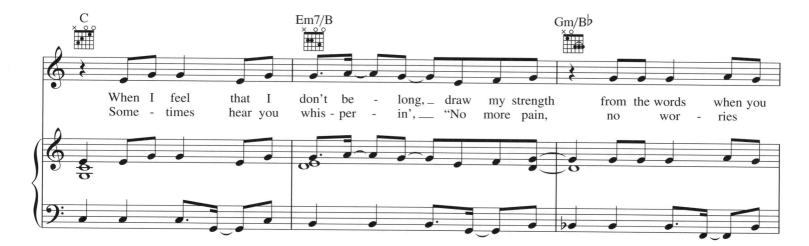

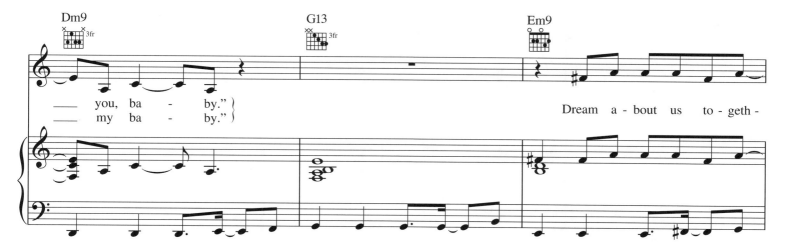

- er a - gain. ___ What I want: us to - geth - er a - gain, ___ ba - by.

But I know we'll be to - geth - er a - gain, ___ 'cause ev - 'ry - where I ___ go,

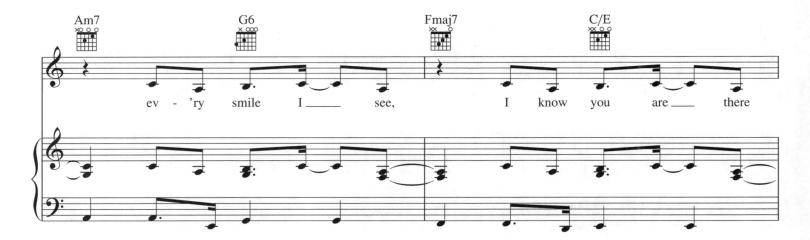

ev - 'ry smile I ___ see, I know you are ___ there

smil - in' back at ___ me. Danc - in' in moon - light,

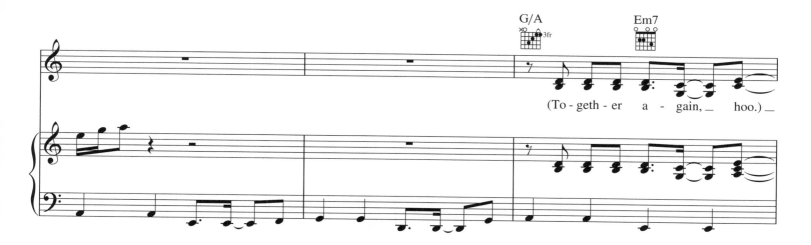

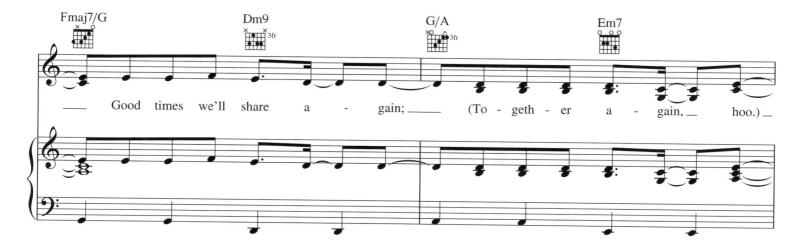

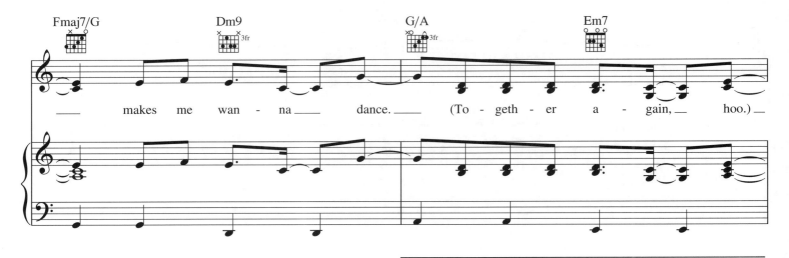

makes me wan - na ___ dance. ___ (To - geth - er a - gain, ___ hoo.) ___

Say it loud and ___ proud; ___ (To - geth - er a - gain, ___ hoo.) ___

___ all my love's for ___ you. ___ (To - geth - er a - gain.) ___

all my love's for ___ you. There are times when I

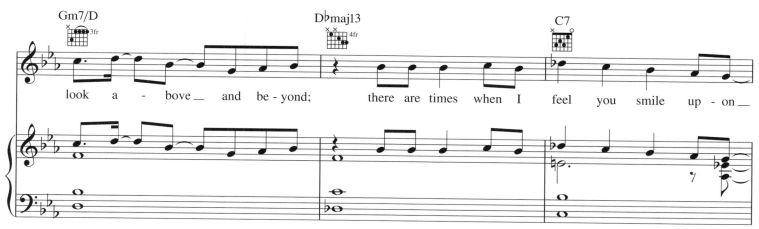

look a - bove __ and be - yond; there are times when I feel you smile up - on __

__ me, ba - by. I'll nev - er for - get __ my ba - by.

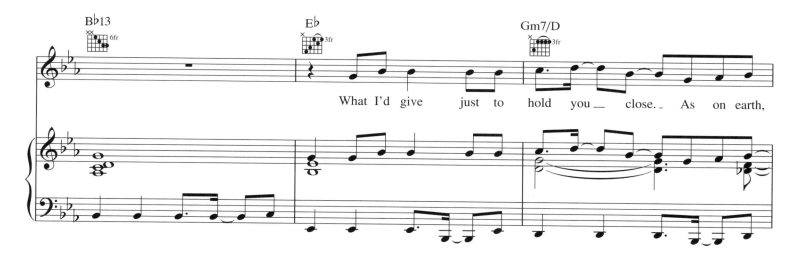

What I'd give just to hold you __ close. __ As on earth,

in heav - en we will be to - geth - er, ba - by,

to-geth - er a - gain, ___ my ba - by.

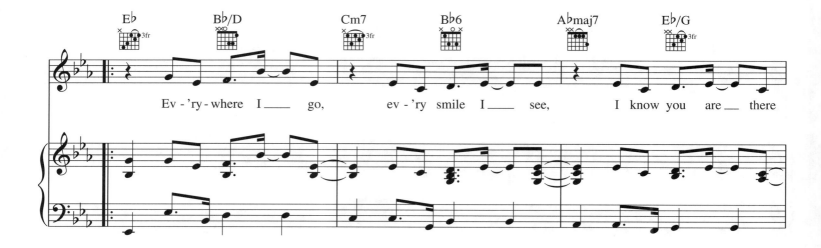

Ev -'ry-where I ___ go, ev -'ry smile I ___ see, I know you are ___ there

smil - in' back at ___ me. Danc - in' in moon - light, I know you are ___ free

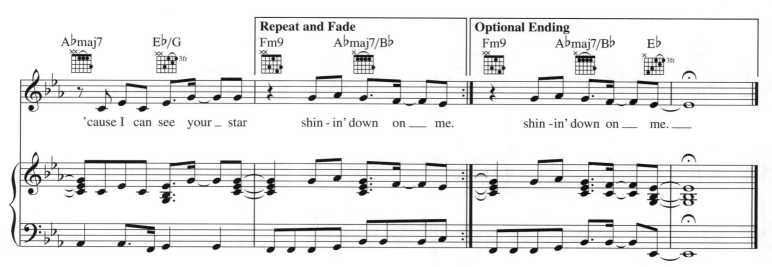

'cause I can see your ___ star shin - in' down on ___ me. shin - in' down on ___ me. ___

WHEN I GET WHERE I'M GOIN'

Words and Music by RIVERS RUTHERFORD
and GEORGE TEREN

spread my wings and fly. I'm gon - na land be - side ___ a

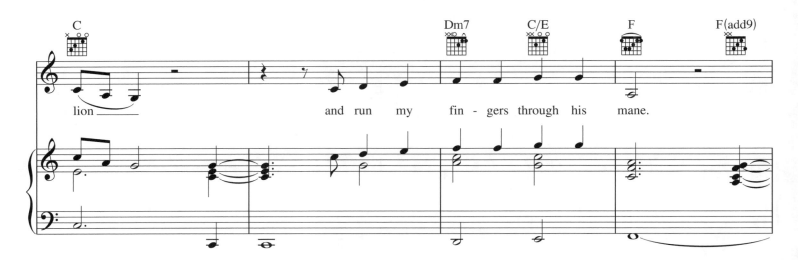

lion ___ and run my fin - gers through his mane.

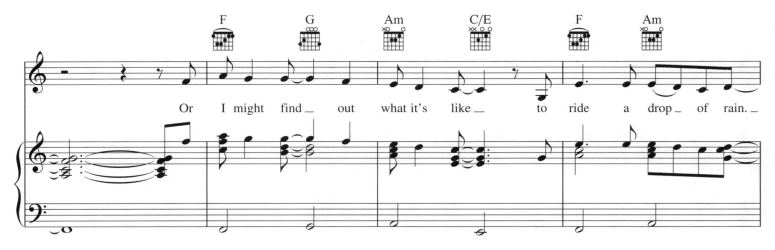

Or I might find ___ out what it's like ___ to ride a drop ___ of rain. ___

___ *Both:* Yeah, when I get where I'm go - in',

there'll be on - ly hap - py tears. ____

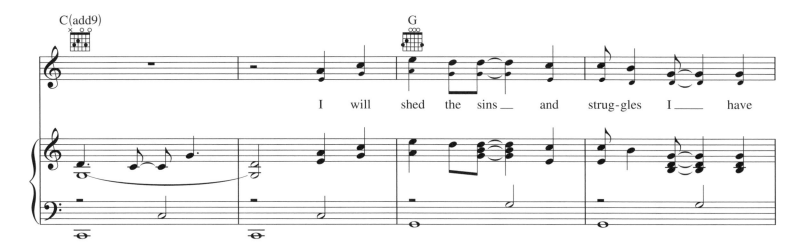

I will shed the sins ____ and strug - gles I ____ have

car - ried all ____ these years. ____ And I'll leave my heart wide o - pen,

I will love and have ____ no fear. ____

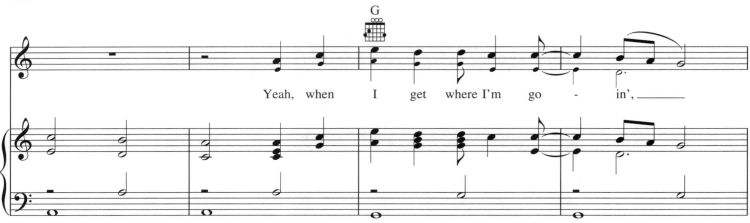

Yeah, when I get where I'm go - in', _____

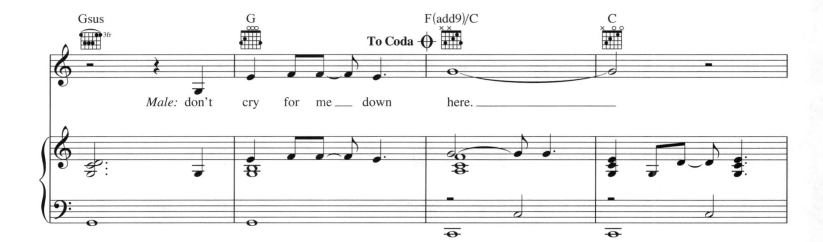

Male: don't cry for me ___ down here. _____

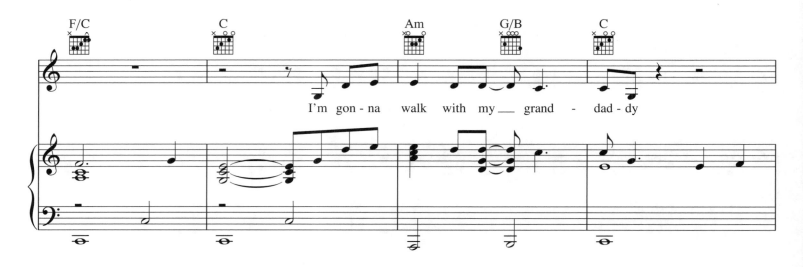

I'm gon - na walk with my ___ grand - dad - dy

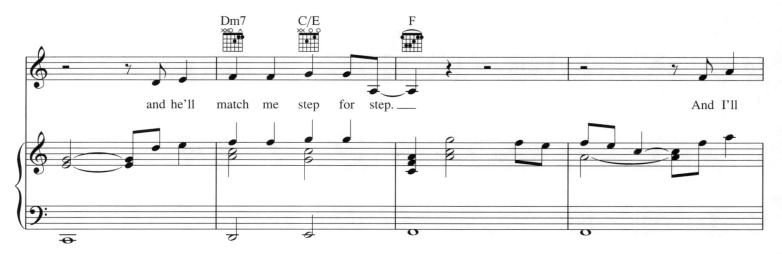

and he'll match me step for step. ___ And I'll

tell him how _ I've missed him ev-'ry min-ute since _ he left. _

And then I'll hug _ his neck. *Both:* Yeah, when

D.S. al Coda

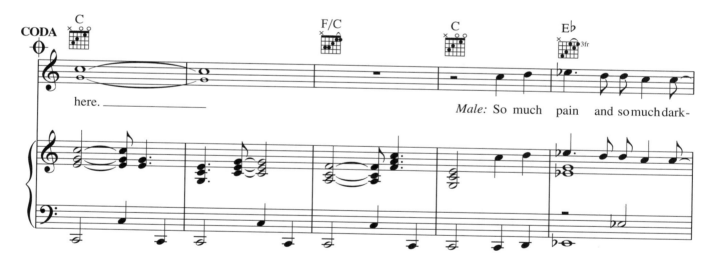

CODA

here. _

Male: So much pain and so much dark-

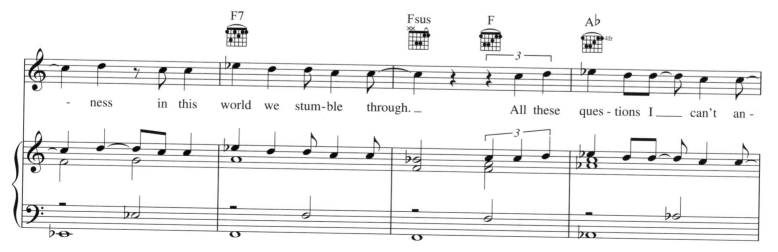

-ness in this world we stum-ble through. _ All these ques-tions I _ can't an-

-swer and so much work to do.

But when I get where I'm go-in',

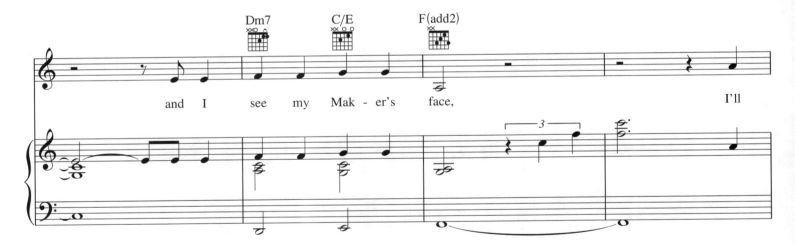

and I see my Mak-er's face, I'll

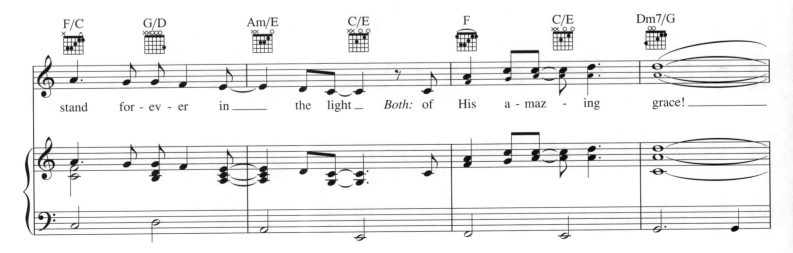

stand for-ev-er in the light _Both:_ of His a-maz-ing grace!

Both: Yeah, when I _____ get where I'm

go - in'. _____

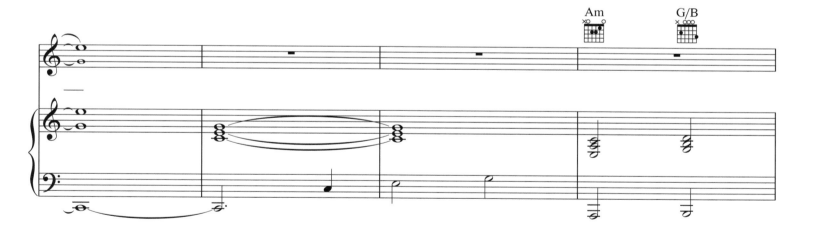

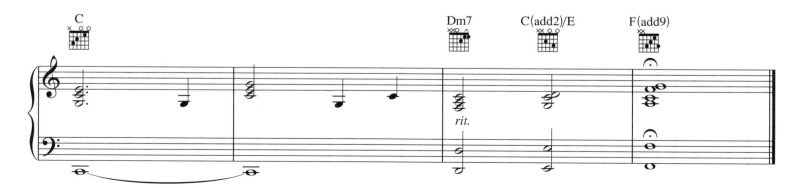

rit.

WHEN I REACH THE PLACE I'M GOING

Words and Music by EMORY GORDY JR.
and JOE HENRY

When I reach the place I'm
light be-gins with
hands to hold our

go - ing, I will sure - ly know my
dark - ness, ev - 'ry flow - er is once a
sor - row, we have tears to heal the

way. And I will turn and look in-
seed. And with the sun and wind to
pain. And though your eyes ask man - y

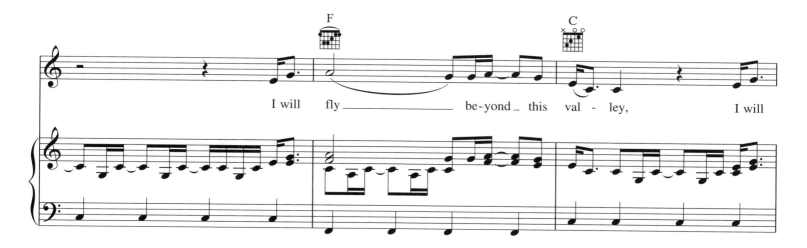

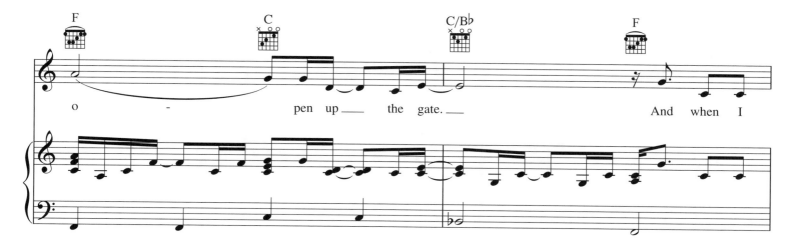

reach   the place _ I'm   go - ing, ___   I will

sure - ly know _ my ___ way.

D.S. al Coda

We have

CODA

_ name.   I was born _____ with-out __ a whis -

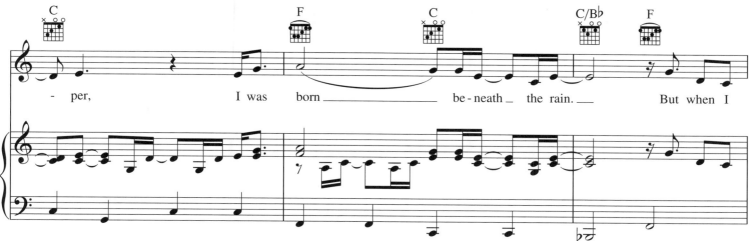

-per, I was born _____ be-neath _ the rain. ___ But when I

reach the place _ I'm go - ing, ___ I will

sure - ly know _ my ____ way. I will

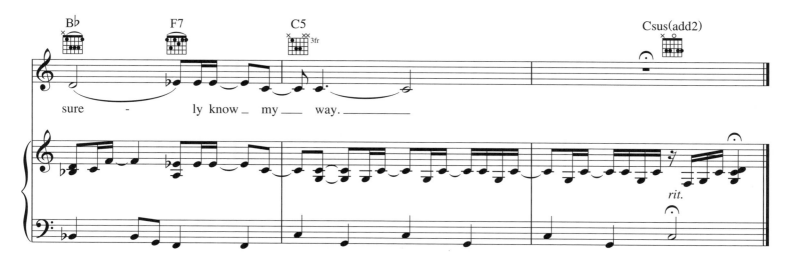

sure - ly know _ my __ way. _____

WHEN THE RIVER MEETS THE SEA

Words and Music by
PAUL WILLIAMS

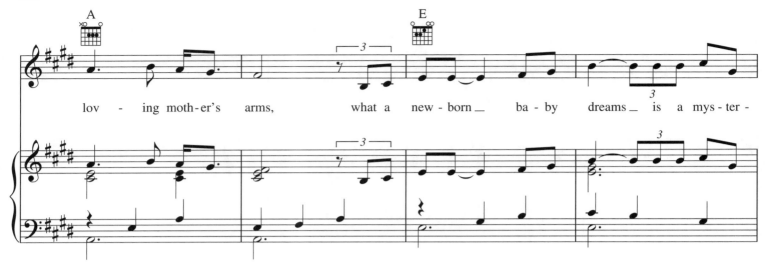

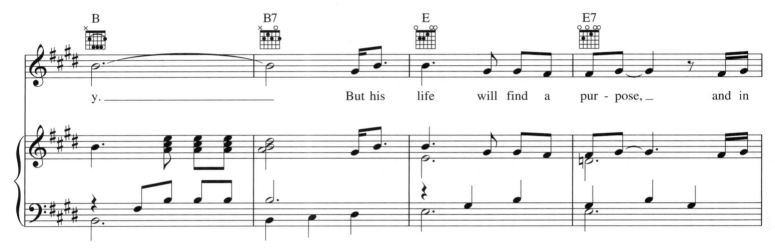

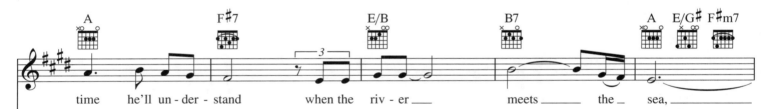

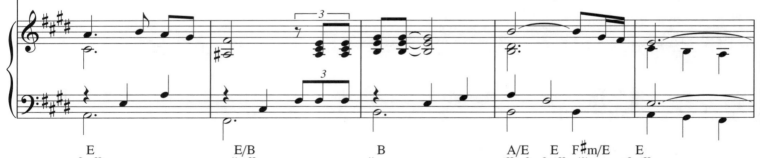

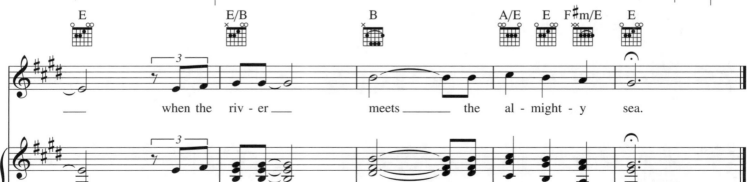

WHO YOU'D BE TODAY

Words and Music by WILLIAM LUTHER
and AIMEE MAYO

Moderately fast

Sun-ny days seem to hurt the most. ___ I wear the pain like a

see the world, would you chase your dreams? ___ Set-tle down with a

heav-y coat. ___ I feel you ev-'ry-where ___ I go. ___

fam-i-ly? ___ I won-der what would you name your ba-

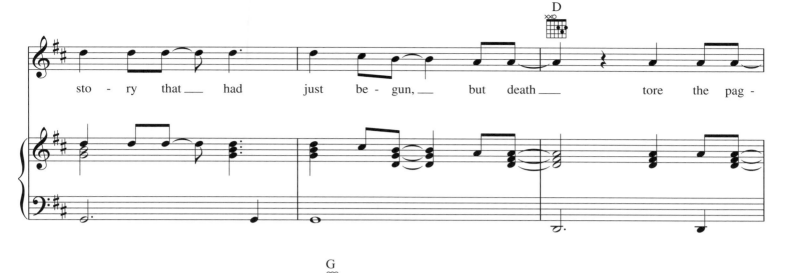

sto - ry that ___ had just be - gun, ___ but death ___ tore the pag -

- es all ___ a - way. ___

God knows how I ___ miss you. ___ All the hell that I've ___

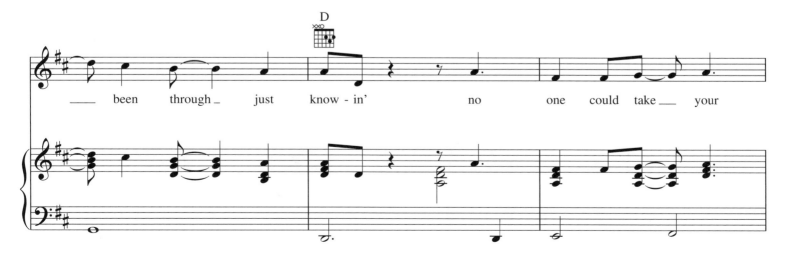

___ been through ___ just know - in' no one could take ___ your

place.   Some - times ___   I won - der

To Coda

who you'd   be ___   to - day. ___

D.S. al Coda

Would you

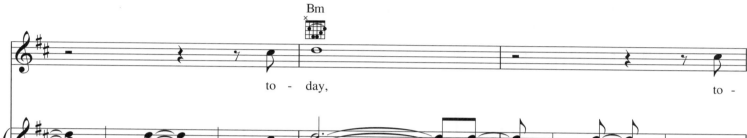

To - day,

to - day,   to -

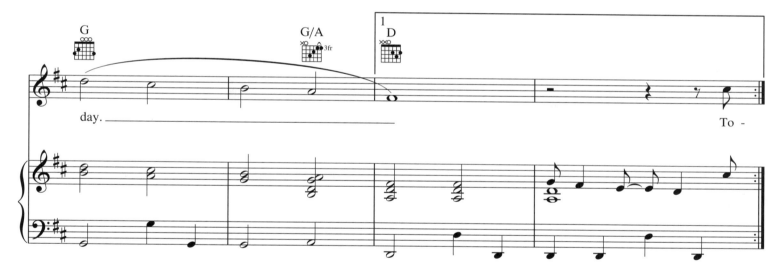

day. _____   To -

Sun - ny days seem to hurt the most. ___ I wear the pain like a

heav - y coat. ___ The on - ly thing that gives ___ me hope ___

is I know ___ I'll

see you a - gain ___ some - day,

some - day,

some -

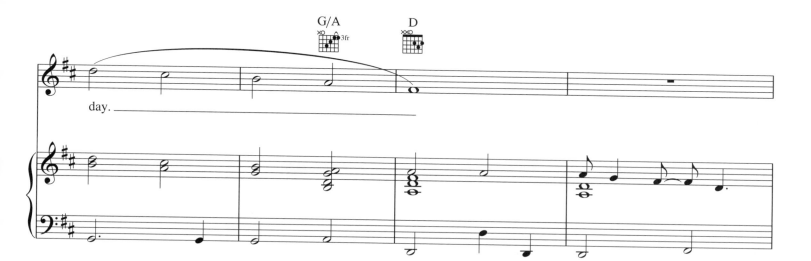

day. _____

WHO KNEW

Words and Music by ALECIA MOORE,
MAX MARTIN and LUKASZ GOTTWALD

Moderately fast

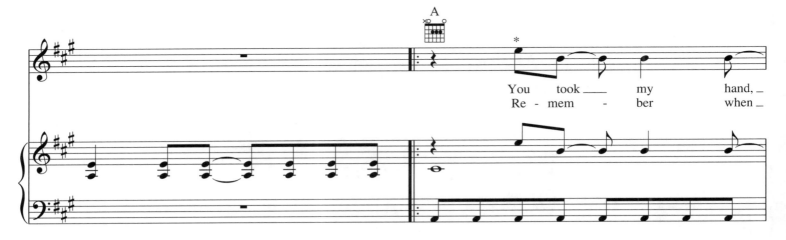

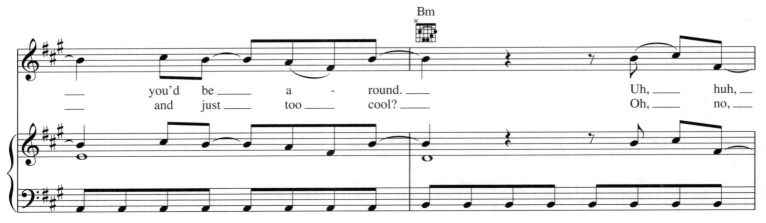

* Vocal is written one octave higher than sung.

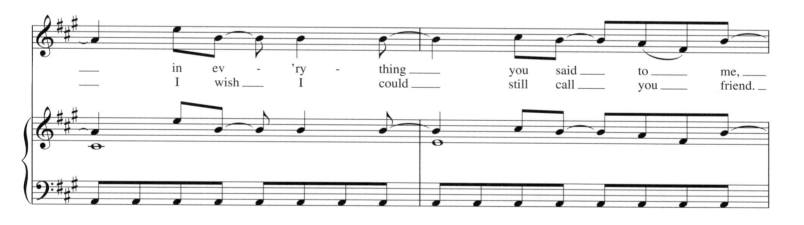

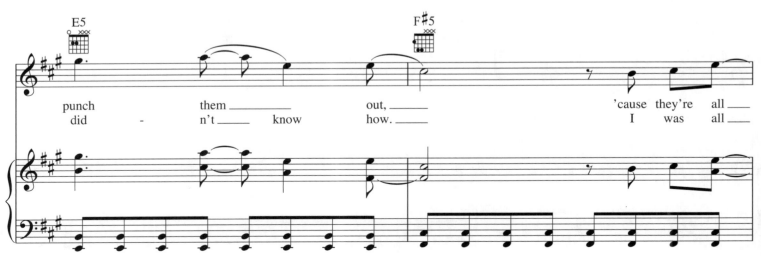

wrong. ___ I ___ know bet - ter,
wrong, ___ but they ___ knew bet - ter.

'cause ___ } you said ___ for - ev - er and ev - er.
Still, ___ }

Who ___ knew? _____

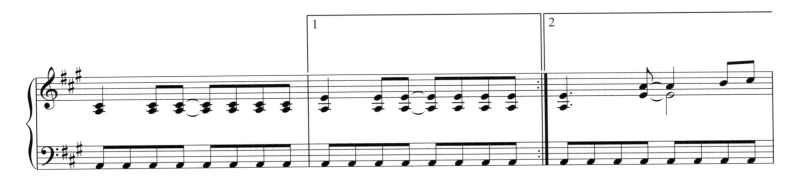

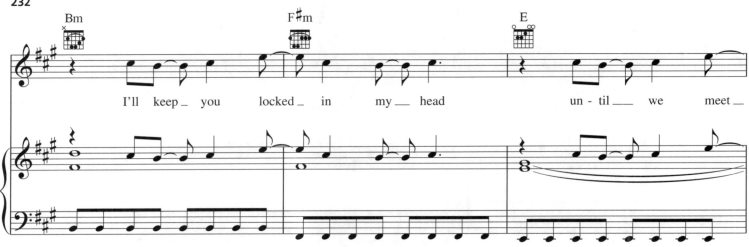

I'll keep __ you locked __ in my __ head un - til __ we meet __

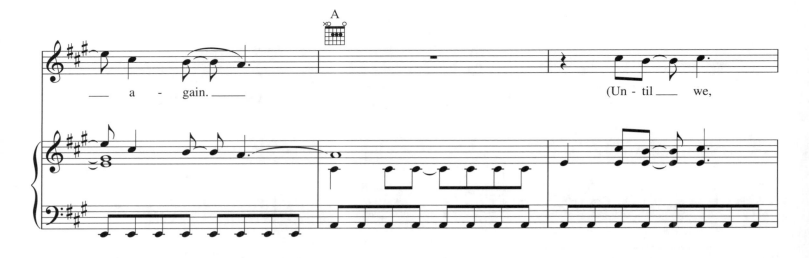

__ a - gain. __ (Un - til __ we,

un - til __ we meet __ a - gain.) __ And I won't __ for - get __

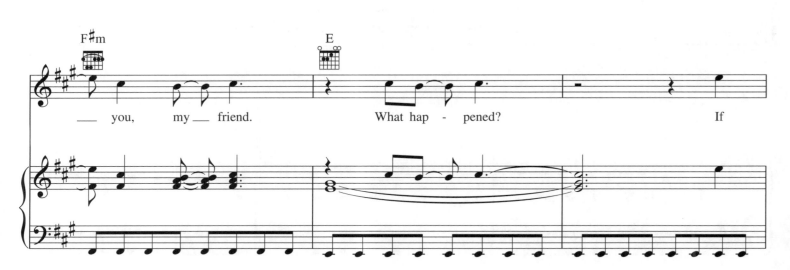

__ you, my __ friend. What hap - pened? If

some - one __ said three years __ from now __ you'd be long __

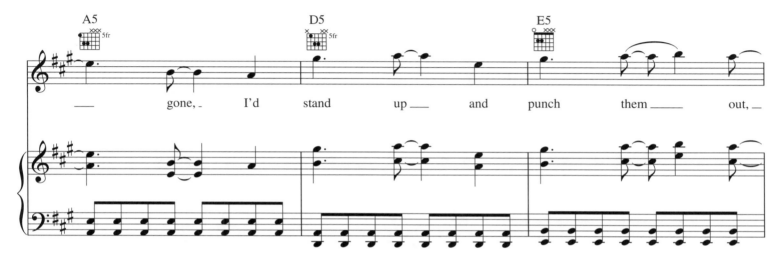

__ gone, __ I'd stand up __ and punch them _____ out, __

__ 'cause they're all _____ wrong, __ and

that last __ kiss I'll cher - ish un - til __ we meet __

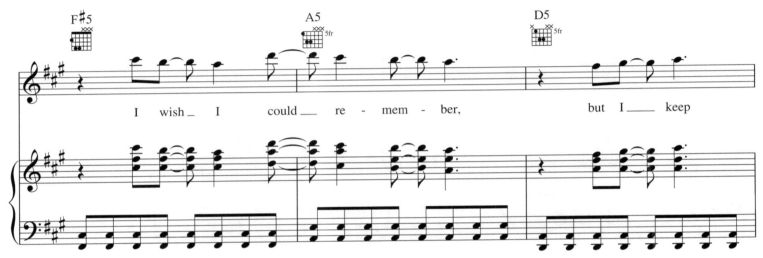

My dar - ling, my dar - ling, who __ knew?

My dar - ling, I miss __ you, my dar - ling.

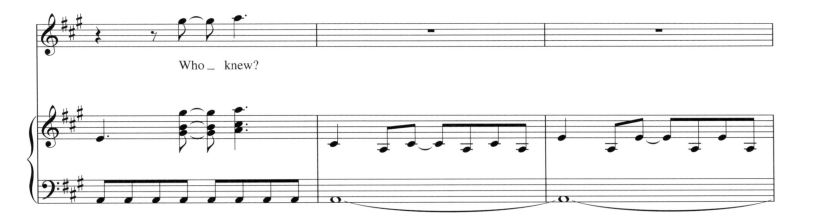

Who __ knew?

Who __ knew?

WISHING YOU WERE SOMEHOW HERE AGAIN

from THE PHANTOM OF THE OPERA

Music by ANDREW LLOYD WEBBER
Lyrics by CHARLES HART
Additional Lyrics by RICHARD STILGOE

Andante

CHRISTINE: You were once my one com-pan-ion, you were all that mat-tered. You were once a friend and fa-ther, then my world was shat-tered.

dream-ing of you won't help me to do all that you dreamed I

Poco meno mosso

could. Three long years I've knelt in si-lence,

held your mem-'ry near me. Three long years of

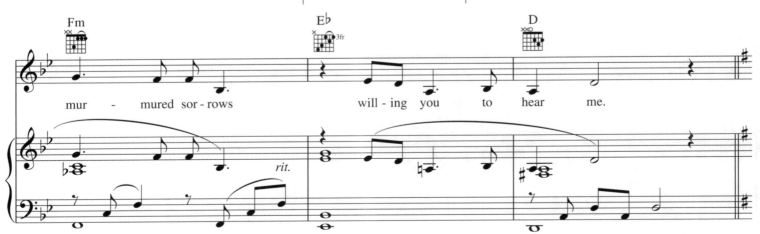

mur-mured sor-rows will-ing you to hear me.